The Emigrant Letters, A Family Story Revealed

DEDICATION

This book is dedicated to the memory of my cousin, Robert Schlichting (1950-2023), who carefully preserved the Schlichting letters in Oregon and, for too few years, was my collaborator in the project that inspired this book.

The
Emigrant Letters

A Family Story Revealed

Merlin Schlichting

The Emigrant Letters, A Family Story Revealed © 2024
Merlin Schlichting

All rights reserved. You may not use or reproduce any part of this book in any manner whatsoever without the author's written permission, except for brief quotations included in critical articles and reviews.

The author and the publisher distribute the information in this book on an "as is" basis, without warranty. Even though the author and publisher have taken every precaution in preparing this work, they do not have any liability to any person or entity for any loss or damage caused or alleged to be caused directly or indirectly by the information in this book.

First Printing: September 2024
First Edition

Paperback: 978-1-955541-51-0
eBook: 978-1-955541-52-7
Hardcover: 978-1-955541-53-4
LCCN: 2024918831

Interior and cover design by Ann Aubitz
Photos are from the author's collection unless otherwise noted.

Published by FuzionPress
1250 E 115th Street
Burnsville, MN 55337
fuzionpress.com
612-781-2815

Acknowledgments

Hildegard Schmoelcke of Hohenwestedt, Germany, a relative I first met in 2019, provided documents and letters and helped with deciphering difficult handwriting. My cousin Madeline Kingsley provided copies of letters she had scanned. She also took on the unenviable task of proofreading my writing. David Schlichting, my brother and author of the *Hinrich* book, provided photos, along with numerous insights gained during the extensive research he undertook for his book. Elanna Schlichting of Oregon continues to search for more letters that might yet be discovered among old family papers kept there. They and others all encouraged me to pursue the writing of this book. My thanks to them all.

The land belongs to the future...We come and go, but the land is always here. And the people who love it and understand it are the people who own it—for a little while.
~Willa Cather

TABLE OF CONTENTS

Introduction		9
Chapter 1	The Setting: Neuland in the Oste Dike region of Germany, Emigration to America	11
Chapter 2	**1867-1870** **Arriving in America: The First Minnesota Farm, First Letters from the Old Country**	17
Chapter 3	**Letters from 1871** **Sorrow and Loss**	29
Chapter 4	**1873-1875** **Productive Years in Minnesota, Hard Years in the Old Country**	37
Chapter 5	**1876-1877** **The Move West Begins**	53

Chapter 6	1878-1879 Oregon!	69
Chapter 7	1880 A Notable Death and Two Weddings, Transitions	83
Chapter 8	1881-1885 Oregon Ventures: An Untimely Death, Changes for the Oste Dike Family	93
Chapter 9	1886-1904 The Passing of a Generation	101
Chapter 10	1905 and Beyond The Next Generation and the Tie that Binds	119
Sources		133

INTRODUCTION

In a time when writing letters by hand has nearly become a lost art, and when receiving even one such letter is a notable occasion, having access to a small library of old handwritten letters from our forebears is something that is both rare and a treasure.

Descendants of Hinrich and Caroline Schlichting are privileged to have access to numerous letters of their forebears that were written from the 1860s into the early 20th century. Many letters were written between Hinrich and his siblings in the U.S. after their immigration in the 1860s. Many others were sent by relatives still in Germany to these new Americans.

While many of the letters in the collection were kept by the Schlichting family in Oregon, others have come from different locations or individuals. And while many of the letters or documents are in their original state, in some cases, only copies are available. Overall, they have been given the name, The Schlichting Letters Collection. With a few exceptions, the letters under consideration for this work include the years 1867 through 1919.

Together with a personal journal written by Johann Schlichting (1844-1883), a memoir by John August Schlichting (1885-1968), and previously published writings, they form the library of information that have made this work possible, as they reveal insights into the early years of our Schlichting family in the United States.

Who Wrote the Letters?

There were at least ten family members involved in writing the letters in this collection, including the following:

In the U.S.
- Johann (I) Schlichting (1810-1880).[1]
- Hinrich Schlichting (1837-1904), Johann I and his wife Elisabeth's oldest son.

- Caroline (Truebenbach) Schlichting (1853-1930), Hinrich's wife.
- Claus Schlichting (1840-1915), Hinrich's brother.
- Johann (II) Schlichting (1844-1883), Hinrich's brother.
- Rebecka (Schlichting) Matthiesen (1853-1895), Hinrich's sister.
- Anton Schlichting (1854-1871), Hinrich's youngest brother.

In Germany, in the Oste Dike Region,[2] the communities of Neuland and Breitenwisch
- Peter Schlichting (1833-1894), Johann I's brother.
- Diedrich Schlichting (1815-1883), also a brother of Johann I.
- Metta (Schlichting) Hellwege (1835-1919), sister of Johann I.
- Anton Blank (1828-1916), Johann I's brother-in-law (Elisabeth's younger brother) and favorite uncle of Johann I and Elisabeth's children.

Letters or other documents from people other than family members are also included. Letters sent by the American family to their relatives in Germany have not survived, but it is obvious that letters traveled in both directions. Frequently, the German relatives mentioned a topic or event that the Americans had written about, and on several occasions, they thanked their American relatives for the money they had sent.

Merlin Schlichting
Roseville, Minnesota
July, 2024

---

[1] This Johann Schlichting (1810-1880) is assigned the "I" to distinguish him from his son, also Johann (1844-1883), who is assigned a "II".
[2] The significance of the name "Oste Dike" is described in Chapter 1.

Chapter 1
The Setting
Neuland in the Oste Dike region of Germany, Emigration to America

For Hinrich Schlichting, his siblings, and their parents Johann I and Elisabeth, home was a small farm along the dike on the east side of the Oste River in the village of Neuland. The English equivalent of Neuland would be "New-Land." This refers to the fact that its primary feature was farmland that had been won from the sea and the marshy lowlands of the region. The Oste River meanders northward through this flat expanse as it flows toward the Elbe River estuary, bound on both banks by high dikes.

The name "Oste Dike" derives from its setting.[3] To this day, the topography of the area is defined by the river and its dikes, and by numerous locks, dams, sluices, and canals. The farm fields that have been won from the surrounding marsh look like long, raised strips of land. They are 30 to 40 yards across and 100 or more yards long. These strips are called polders;[4] it is on them that farmers grow crops and graze livestock. The polders are raised lengthways along the middle, sloping down toward each side. Each polder is separated from the next by a narrow waterway—a ditch—where runoff water is collected and channeled toward sluices and then canals that carry it to locks. During ebb tide the locks are opened and the water in the canal is drawn by tidal flow via a channel under the dike, into the Oste River and toward the mouth of the river.

A lengthwise view of polders in the Oste Dike area. Each polder is sloped toward the edges, where water drains into ditches. From there it is channeled toward the locks and eventually the river. The Oste River flows beyond the distant line of trees.

---

[3] The Oste Dike region (in German, *Ostedeich*) includes the Oste River and its dikes. The region is located roughly between the Weser River to the west and the Elbe River to the east and north. The Oste River meanders through the region from south to north, eventually emptying in the estuary of the Elbe River near the North Sea. Throughout the region the river is held within bounds by nearly 20-foot-high dikes on both banks. The dikes protect the low-lying land, farms, and towns from flooding. Throughout the Oste Dike region, the flow of the river is heavily influenced by ocean tides. During the build-up to high tide, it actually flows *upstream*, filling with water, while at low tide it flows downstream toward the sea, taking excess water with it.

[4] "Polder" comes from the Dutch name for these features. The Germans also know them as polders, but they more often call them "parcels" (*Stücke*) or simply "fields" (*Felder*).

Without this complicated system of water management, it would be nearly impossible to farm or even to live in the area. Indeed, even with dikes, locks, and canals, strong storms occasionally blow in from the North Sea and cause serious flood damage, up to and including damage to the dikes and locks themselves. Life in the Oste Dike area has always been both hard and precarious. But the rich quality of the soil has also allowed farmers there to earn a good living, as long as overall conditions remain favorable.

Johann I and Elisabeth Schlichting lived in Neuland just east of the dike (on the "inner" dike side, the side farthest from the river). The farm belonged to the Blanks, Elisabeth's birth family.[5] Elisabeth's mother, Ilse, had been born a Jungclaus and had grown up on the much larger Jungclaus heritage farm next door.[6] The Jungclaus and Blank farms were within easy walking distance of each other by way of the road that ran along the base of the inner dike. The Blank—later Schlichting—farm was smaller and most likely consisted of only two polder widths, perhaps 20 acres.[7]

---

[5] In some documents, the name is spelled "Blanck."
[6] The heritage farm has been in Jungclaus family ownership since the mid-1600s. As of 2023, Heinz Jungclaus has been the owner for more than 50 years.
[7] This is a generous estimate. It is based on Johann II's journal (Part 1, p. 19), where he wrote that in 1863, when he and his brother Claus could find no carpentry work, they went home in late summer, where "...we helped father in the fields (polders). Our main work was to turn over [the soil] of the two dike polders with a shovel (Johann's German: *unser Hauptwerk war dass wir die 2 deich stücken mit der Schaufel umgruben*). (See footnote #4 regarding polders.) This was backbreaking work. Having seen the polders on that Oste Dike site today, I am estimating the total area of the two polders to be roughly 20 acres. Land available for raising crops would have been less than that, since some land would have been kept as pasture for the livestock. This journal segment is also in *New World Beginnings* on p. 20 but is inaccurately translated.

View from atop the Oste River dike, looking north (downstream). The farm of Johann I and Elisabeth Schlichting was to the right (east) of the dike, very close to this point. Sheep (seen mid-picture) are grazed along the dike to control vegetation and to keep the soil conditioned and fertilized.

As noted above, when they married in 1837, Johann I and Elisabeth lived with her parents Claus and Ilse and her younger brother Anton on the smaller farm. Johann worked with his father-in-law Claus farming the land, keeping the water ditches clear, and tending the livestock. Claus Blank died in 1843, and thereafter Johann I became the owner. Elisabeth's mother, Ilse, continued to live with them until her death in 1865. Elisabeth's brother, Anton Blank, was just nine years old in 1837. He lived with the family until they emigrated years later. It is correct to say that he grew up among his nephews and nieces. He also became a favorite uncle and was accorded the affectionate name of "Onkel Tönnes" (akin to "Uncle Tony").[8]

The first child of Johann I and Elisabeth's was born September 12, 1837 and was named Hinrich.[9] Elisabeth would eventually give birth to nine children. Of those, only four lived into adulthood: Hinrich, Claus, Johann II, and Rebecka. A fourth son, Anton, lived until shortly after his 17th birthday. Elisabeth herself died in Neuland in May 1866 at age 51. The parish record stated that she died of congestive heart disease.

---

[8] At the very beginning of his journal, Johann II related three anecdotes that included his "Onkel Tönnes," all from when Johann was just three years old, so around 1847. "Tönnes" is a diminutive of Anton, which in turn is short for Antonius.
[9] The baptismal entry listed his name as "Heinrich," but he always used "Hinrich."

1866-1867[10]

The year 1866 was momentous for the family. After Elisabeth's death in May, Johann I bore sole responsibility for his two youngest children, Rebecka, age 14, and Anton, who in July turned 12. His three oldest sons, Hinrich, Claus, and Johann II, were all in their twenties. All three of them had learned the carpentry trade and were working at various job sites in the region. This choice turned out to be wise, but initially it was mostly practical. Given the very small size of the family's farm, and the size of the family, its viability as an ongoing enterprise seemed very unlikely for even one of the sons, to say nothing of four. Thus, learning the carpentry trade at least made it possible for the three older sons to support themselves and help to pay expenses on the farm. Johann II's journal is filled with reports of the three brothers working for numerous neighbors on building projects, also at a shipbuilding yard in Bremerhaven. But often there simply was no work. During such times, they would return to the farm to help their father in the field or with livestock and to make improvements to the house.

In his journal, Johann II reported that even before his oldest brother Hinrich's discharge in spring 1865 from compulsory military service for the Kingdom of Hanover, he was able to return home for longer periods of time. In fall 1864 Hinrich was accepted at a trade school and completed the course for carpentry, graduating as a journeyman carpenter in March of 1865. At the time, Hinrich was 28 years old. In June of 1866 he applied for and was issued a travel pass (*Reisepass*). From a later letter by his father Johann I, we learn that it had been Hinrich's intention to emigrate, and that his father Johann I hoped to follow.[11] In late June 1866, several weeks after his mother's death, Hinrich left for America. He settled in Cincinnati, Ohio, and began to work as a carpenter.

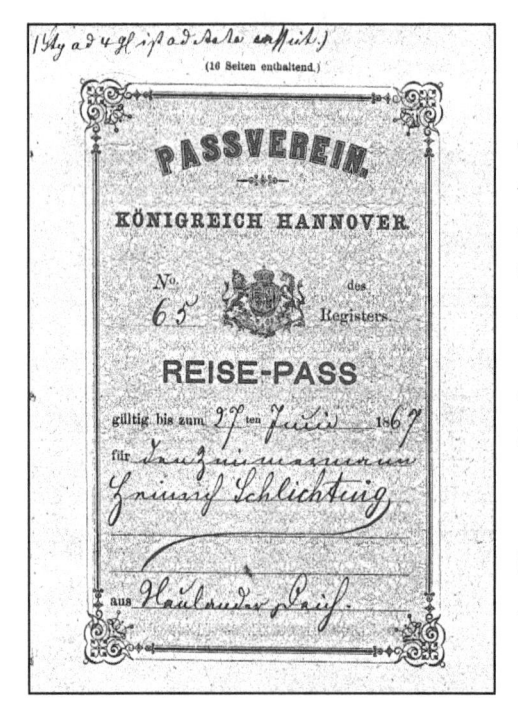

The first page of Hinrich's Travel Pass (Reise-Pass). It was issued June 27, 1866, and was valid for one year. The text reads: "Pass Association, Kingdom of Hanover, No. 65. Travel Pass, valid until 27 June 1867, for the journeyman carpenter Heinrich Schlichting, of Haulander Dike (where Hinrich was working at the time)." Further pages gave his age as 28, his build as "tall," hair color, "dark blond," eye color, "gray" and facial shape, "oval." No other physical features were noted. "Heinrich" was his given name, but he always used "Hinrich." He signed this document as "H. Schlichting."

Source: Dorothy Schlichting collection. Translation by Uwe Stock, Lensahn, Germany, and Merlin Schlichting. Also in *Hinrich*, p. 30

---

[10] For a more detailed analysis of the overall setting in Germany at this time, as well as the family's situation, see David Schlichting's book *Hinrich, Annals of an Immigrant Family 1866-1913*. Memoir Books, Chico, CA, 2015, especially Chapter 1. From here on, references to the book will read simply *Hinrich*.

[11] The letter, written in Minnesota in October 1871, will be discussed in Chapter 3.

Talk of emigration continued among the rest of the family. In the spring of 1865 Johann II, then 21, had been drafted and was serving in the Hanoverian army, while 25-year-old Claus continued working carpentry jobs. Johann was assigned to the infantry of the Hanoverian Guard Regiment (*Garde-Regiment*)—the same regiment in which his brother Hinrich had served. Unlike his older brother, however, Johann II saw active duty when his regiment was engaged at the Battle of Langensalza on June 27, 1866, between the armies of Hanover and Prussia. As the saying goes, Hanover won the battle but lost the war. The Prussian forces proved overwhelming, and within days after the battle, the Kingdom of Hanover ceased to exist. In early July, Johann II and other members of the regiment were placed on indefinite leave (*auf unbestimmte Zeit beurlaubt*) after swearing they would not take up arms against the king of Prussia. Johann then returned home. By the time he arrived in Neuland in early July, Hinrich had already left for America.

Johann II and Claus spent the summer and fall working carpentry jobs, though employment was hard to find. In his journal, Johann II wrote that during that time he was ordered to register for service in the Prussian army.[12] Thereupon, he and Claus began making serious plans to emigrate the following spring.[13] Then in November of 1866, Johann II was ordered to report for duty in the Prussian army. This he was unwilling to do, and the result was that Johann made a mad dash to flee the country and escape to America. With no papers[14] and just a few personal belongings, Johann II, with Claus' help, left home during the night of Nov. 16-17 and headed for the harbor at Bremerhaven. After borrowing money from a former employer for passage on a ship, Johann II bought a ticket and boarded a sailing ship named the *Emilie*—not the steamship he had hoped to take. On November 21 the ship set sail for America. The voyage was a near disaster, and it left Johann with significant health issues. He did not arrive in New York until February 23, 1867, shortly after his 23rd birthday. He wrote details of the ordeal in his journal.[15]

Meanwhile, Claus, by then 26, left for America in late December 1866 and arrived in New York in January 1867, a whole month earlier than Johann. Finally, in late February 1867, Claus and Johann II were reunited with older brother Hinrich in Cincinnati. There, they sought to establish themselves in the carpentry trade. Their training and experience as carpenters now proved to be of vital importance.

The three sons were able to keep their father in Germany informed of their whereabouts and welfare, though as stated above, none of the letters sent back to Germany have survived. Evidence of their correspondence is found in the earliest letter of the family we still have. It was written by Father Johann I from Neuland on July 8, 1868. He sent it to Hinrich in Cincinnati. In it, he referred to a letter Hinrich had sent.

In the letter, Johann I expressed satisfaction with the price he had negotiated for the sale of the Neuland farm. He advised Hinrich—and by extension Claus and Johann II as well—to study American law and finances and to be careful with the money they earned. Anticipating his own

---

[12] The Kingdom of Prussia had defeated the Hanoverians in mid-1866 and assumed power in the former Kingdom of Hanover.
[13] Johann II Schlichting op. cit., p. 7. Also printed in *New World Beginnings*, p. 27
[14] Johann II (or perhaps his father) had applied for a copy of his baptismal certificate as a form of identification, thinking to use it when he planned to leave the next spring. But the document wasn't issued until November 22, by which time Johann II had already left. The certificate survives. Most likely, his father Johann I brought it with him when he immigrated in 1869.
[15] Johann II Schlichting, op. cit., pp. 7-11. It is also described in *Hinrich*, Chapter 2, and it appears as well in *New World Beginnings* pp. 27-29.

departure for America soon, he urged them to find "an area where we can prosper without having to earn our money all over again." That area's location would come to light in the course of the following months.

In this same letter, Johann I also wrote that his son Johann (II) had been awarded a medal of honor from former Hanoverian King George V, for his service in the Hanoverian army, particularly at the Battle of Langensalza in June 1866. Father Johann wrote that he had the medal at his home. Whether he brought it with him to America is not known. There is no record of it in family documents.

CHAPTER 2
1867-1870

Arriving in America: The First Minnesota Farm
First Letters from the Old Country

Date	Source	Writer in Germany / Recipient	Writer in U.S. / Recipient	Comments
1866 June, Hinrich arrived in America, settled in Cincinnati.					
1867 January, Claus arrived in New York. **1867 February, Johann II arrived. Claus and Johann II joined Hinrich in Cincinnati.**					
1867, Dec. 22	transcription of original		Johann II Schlichting to unknown recipient	Johann's brief description of leaving home in Nov. 1866 and arriving in Bremerhaven.
1868 May, Claus and Johann II moved to Chicago briefly, then to Milwaukee. Hinrich remained in Cincinnati.					
1868, July	photocopy	Johann I Schlichting, Neuland, to Hinrich Schlichting, Cincinnati		Family land in Neuland, Germany, had been sold, but Johann I wouldn't leave until all money had been received. Johann II awarded medal of honor for wartime service.
1869 June, Hinrich accompanied Johann I, Rebecka, and Anton from Germany to America, joined Claus and Johann II in Milwaukee. Cousin Johann Jungclaus traveled on the same ship to America.					
1869	prov. by Hildegard Schmoelcke		Johann Jungclaus, Milwaukee maybe, to unknown recipient	A description of Johann J's 1869 voyage to and arrival in the U.S. and the train trip to Milwaukee.
1869 Fall, Hinrich, Johann I, Rebecka, and Anton moved from Milwaukee to Wabasha County, Minnesota.					
1869, Nov. 26	original	Peter Schlichting, Breitenwisch, to Johann I Schlichting, Minnesota.		Day of Prayer not well attended. His and Joh I's father Hinrich (1785-1874) relieved of dike reeve duties. Earthquake. Crop prices, neighborhood news. Letter condition fragile.
1870 June, Hinrich purchased 160 acres of land in Wabasha County, Minnesota for $1,500 (Parcel A).					
1870, Jun. 5	original	Peter Schlichting, Brtnw. to Johann I Schlichting & family, Minn.		Spring planting was done, but a late frost killed seedlings. Big horse sale by raffle in Stade. Neighborhood land sale controversy. Peter tried to help two men, Hinrich & Johann Blank.
1870, Oct. 3	photocopy		Hinrich S, Minn., to Claus & Johann II S, Milwaukee	They had broken 1/3 of the land they had bought. Reported on their first harvest. Encouraged his brothers to come to Minn. so the family could buy more land.

The Emigrant Letters ♦ 17

1870, Nov.	photocopy	Peter S, Brtnw., to Claus & Johann II S, Milwaukee		Continuing a theme from an earlier letter, he described help given to the unfortunates. Anton Blank was still living in their old farmhouse and had rented some land. An added comment referred to the fall of the French fortress at Metz, Oct. 1870, in Franco-Prussian War.
1870, Nov. 4	original	Peter S, Brtnw., to Johann I S and family, Minn.		Neighborhood news. War news. Peter & Joh. I's nephew Hinrich was a soldier in France. Harvest good, incl. honey. Asked Joh I to write soon. Sent greetings from their father Hinrich & his sisters Anna Margaretha and Metta.

In June of 1866, Hinrich Schlichting, the oldest of the sons of Johann I and Elisabeth Schlichting, emigrated to America, arriving in New York. He traveled on to Cincinnati, Ohio, where he began carpentry work. His younger brothers Claus and Johann II arrived in New York in January and February 1867, respectively. Each of them found his way to join Hinrich in Cincinnati. Soon all were employed in carpentry work.

December 22, 1867, Report of Leaving Neuland, by Johann II

The oldest dated item in the letters collection is a short December 1867 note. It was written by Johann II Schlichting, and it described his leaving the family's farm in Neuland in the night of November 16, 1866, his arrival in Bremerhaven, and on Nov. 19 his boarding the ill-fated sailing ship *Emilie*, bound for America. His original work is no longer present, but a German transcription was found among the papers of John August Schlichting (1885-1968), who was Johann II's nephew. Johann II's purpose for writing this one-page article is not clear, especially seeing as he wrote at its end that he already had written a more detailed description in what he called his diary.[16] That much more detailed description of his flight from Neuland and voyage to America is included in Part 3 of the Johann II Schlichting Journal.

---

[16] What Johann II called a diary (*Tagebuch*) was really a journal, with entries made periodically. That is what it will be called in this work.

July 8, 1868, Letter of Johann I Schlichting, Neuland, to Hinrich Schlichting, Cincinnati, OH

The earliest full letter in our collection was written by Johann I Schlichting in July 1868. It appears in translation in *New World Beginnings* on page 7. A poor-quality photocopy of its original was found in a box that also contained Johann II's journal, as well as several items that apparently had been copied and saved by John August Schlichting and his family. I was able to enhance the photocopy, and my translation of that became the source for this work. It should be noted that it contains some corrections from what was printed in *New World Beginnings*.

Writing on July 8 from his Neuland Oste Dike farm in Germany to his son Hinrich in Cincinnati, Ohio (sons Claus and Johann II had moved on to Milwaukee in June), Johann informed Hinrich that the farm had been sold: "Bartholdt Jungclaus[17] has bought the last for 10,500 Marks. The contract will probably be signed soon. We will sell all and keep nothing in memory." He wrote that he was pleased with the sale price. Once the sale was completed, plans were set in motion for Johann I (then 58) and his two youngest children, Rebecka (16) and Anton (13), to emigrate to America. But he also wrote, "I want to get all the money together, lest we take the journey and leave our money behind..." By late spring 1869 the timing for the journey was favorable. Hinrich (then 32) elected to sail back to Germany to accompany his father and two younger siblings on their emigration voyage. We have no letters to reveal details, but obviously arrangements were made and necessary papers obtained to make this possible.[18] The voyage and overland journey took place in June 1869. The entire family was reunited in Milwaukee on June 26.[19]

There is a side story to their voyage that should be related here. Although none of the Schlichting letters or Johann II's journal mention it, another passenger from Neuland Oste Dike accompanied Johann I, Hinrich, Rebecka and Anton on their voyage. His name was Johann Jungclaus. Born in 1842, he grew up on the Jungclaus heritage farm in Neuland, almost next door to the smaller Schlichting farm. Johann was a second cousin to the Schlichting children on their mother Elisabeth's side. These young people had known each other since childhood.

That Johann Jungclaus came to America on the same ship as the Schlichtings first came to light thanks to Hildegard Schmoelcke. Hildegard is a great-granddaughter of Johann Jungclaus. I have been grateful to meet and become acquainted with her. We are in fact distantly related, thanks to our common Jungclaus ancestry. We met in person in September 2019 when my son Tim and I, along with my brother Dave and his son Ryan visited the Neuland Oste Dike neighborhood and met her and her husband Reinhard. We met at the Jungclaus heritage farm in Neuland—where her great-grandfather grew up—hosted there by current owner Heinz Jungclaus and his partner Helga Dressler.

Hildegard later sent me scans of two documents that her great-grandfather had written, the only documents of his that still exist.[20] The first is a summary of his voyage in 1869. It is more like a journal entry, but I have included it in the letters collection because it identified the date of

---

[17] While his identity cannot be verified precisely, a search of the Jungclaus family tree suggests that this Bartholdt farmed in the neighboring village of Engelschoff.
[18] Johann I had obtained certificates from his parish pastor that verified the birth and baptism dates of his children. Copies of several have survived.
[19] Johann Schlichting II Journal, Pt. 3, p. 15. Also copied in *New World Beginnings*, p. 30. Further information about their trip can be found in *Hinrich*, pp. 39-40.
[20] Hildegard informed me that a trunk containing all of Johann Jungclaus' effects, letters, etc. that had been kept at the Jungclaus farm was thrown out a number of years ago without her knowledge. It is most unfortunate.

his departure from Bremerhaven as June 5, 1869, the same day the Schlichtings left, and on the same ship, the *Hermann*. The ship's passenger manifest included a 27-year-old man named Johann Jung... The last letters of the surname were difficult to decipher, and they had been misread by translators—including John August Schlichting, and for a while myself—as "Jungoldus." As my ability to read the German script improved, and as I considered the Johann Jungclaus summary of his journey that Hildegard had sent, I realized that the name was not "Jungoldus" but rather "Jungclaus."

A comment made by Johann II Schlichting in his journal finally brought things into focus. He wrote, "Near Easter (1870) J [ohann] Jungclaus visited [Claus and me in Milwaukee]. He had come over with father and had been working on a farm. Now he was on his way to Minnesota where our relatives were."[21] Johann Jungclaus did in fact join the Schlichtings in southeastern Minnesota, and he remained with them there until his return to Germany in 1871. Letters from 1870 and 1871 confirm this.

November 26, 1869, Letter of Peter Schlichting, Breitenwisch, to Johann I and family, Minnesota

Johann I and the family would have received this letter from Johann's younger brother Peter in Germany in December. This is the earliest letter in the collection that we have in its original state. As can be seen in the image on the following page, it is in fragile condition; in fact, the last several lines of each of its four pages have disintegrated.

---

[21] Johann II Schlichting, op. cit., p. 16.

Breitenwisch, 26 Novem [ber] 1869

"Dear brother and children, by God's grace we have all up till now been healthy and well kept. We have enjoyed good and peaceful times, and life is proceeding in its usual way. A new Day of Prayer was announced for November 10 of this year as Luther's Day,[22] but not many were in church. I hope that in the future observance of the new Day of Prayer will improve. Father (his and Johann I's father Hinrich) has been relieved of his duties as dike reeve.[23] Hinrich Winter from the Neumann farm will be dike reeve in the future. Throughout the summer and fall we have had a lot of rain and storms. Frosts let..."

The last lines of all four of the letter's pages have disintegrated.

Source: Schlichting Letters Collection: 1869-11-26 Peter S Brtnw to Johann I MN

This is the first of many letters in the collection written by Peter to his brother Johann I and Johann's adult children in America. They were newsy letters and were filled with information that covered an array of topics. Four of his letters are included in this chapter. The letters were certainly welcomed by Johann I and his family, since they were the only tangible link to the family and community they had left behind. As I wrote above, the American Schlichtings also wrote to Peter and others in Germany, but none of those letters have survived. Still, we can sometimes know some of what they wrote about from the content of letters sent later by Peter or other German family members. How frequently letters were sent in either direction would have varied, but one series of letters from Peter in 1874 show him having written at roughly monthly intervals.

At this point, some information about this youngest brother of Johann I is in order. Peter Schlichting, who was born in 1833, and his wife Margrethe lived on a small farm in the village of Breitenwisch. Although it no longer exists, archival records have identified the farm's erstwhile location.[24] Peter's widowed brother Diedrich[25] would soon live there as well. During these years, Peter and his wife also were caring

---

[22] November 10, 1483, was the birthdate of church reformer Martin Luther.
[23] The position of dike reeve (*Deichgraf*) meant having responsibility for keeping dikes and water channels in the reeve's community in good repair. It was a crucially important position in the low-lying area of Neuland Oste Dike, which was prone to flooding from storms coming off the nearby North Sea.
[24] See Google Maps coordinates, 53.647776, 9.281763.
[25] Diedrich's given name was Diederich. But Peter always wrote his name without the middle "e," a practice I follow here.

for his, Diedrich, and Johann I's aging father Hinrich (1785-1874). This was the farm where Johann I also had grown up. He left that farm in 1837 when he married Elisabeth Blank. The young couple lived at her parents' small farm just a few miles away in neighboring Neuland. The two villages border each other, with Breitenwisch being slightly farther east and south. The Breitenwisch farm passed out of our Schlichting family after Peter's death in 1894. He left no heirs.

June 5, 1870, Letter of Peter Schlichting, Breitenwisch to Johann I Schlichting, Minnesota

The next of Peter's letters we have is dated June 5, 1870. It too is an original and is intact, including the mailing envelope. Peter wrote about weather and crops and livestock prices, as well as about a horse sale conducted by raffle. There was a great deal of neighborhood news, including the description of a land sale gone sour due to the intoxication of both buyer and seller at the time the deal was struck. He also related a sad story about two brothers named Blank whom Peter was trying to help. Whether they were related to the Neuland Blank family was not indicated.

October 3, 1870, Letter of from Hinrich Schlichting, MN, to his brothers Claus and Johann II, Milwaukee, WI

Between the second and third of Peter's letters in this group is one written by Hinrich. Hinrich wrote from the family's newly purchased land in southeastern Minnesota to his brothers Claus and Johann II, who at the time were working as carpenters in Milwaukee. The letter exists only as a photocopy and is dated October 3.

After Hinrich had brought his father, sister and brother over to America in June 1869 and the whole family was reunited in Milwaukee, he learned about "new" prairie land to farm in southeastern Minnesota. In his journal, Johann II wrote that Hinrich made several exploratory trips to the area and "found a farm to rent...in an area he found to be generally good."[26] Sometime that fall, Hinrich, his father Johann I and the two youngest children, Rebecka and Anton, moved to that land in Wabasha County and began farming on rented land.[27] In June 1870 they bought 160 acres of unbroken prairie land in the neighboring township and near the village of Jacksonville.[28] This was new land, at least in the sense that it had never been farmed the way Europeans—and Americans—practiced farming. Until 1851, however, the land had been home to the Dakota people.

---

[26] Johann II Schlichting, op. cit., p. 15.
[27] See *Hinrich*, pp. 79-83 for more information.
[28] The land is referred to as Parcel A. Much more can be read about it in *Hinrich*, Chapter 6. While Jacksonville no longer exists, its erstwhile location is noted by a small sign along County Road 2. See Google Maps coordinates 44.345802, -92.330719.

"New" Land?

The land in southeastern Minnesota that Hinrich bought in June 1870 (named Parcel A in *Hinrich*) was virgin prairie land that had never seen a plow. It was in Wabasha County, Gillford Township, near Lake City. Hinrich was not the first European-American owner of that quarter-section (160 acres). At least two other parties—absentee landowners in Ohio—had owned it since it first was surveyed in 1856.

Until 1851, that same land had been home to the Mdewakanton and Wahpekute bands of Dakota Sioux. By the 1851 treaties of Traverse des Sioux and Mendota, the Dakota bands living west of the Mississippi River ceded some 24 million acres of land in present-day Minnesota, South Dakota, and Iowa to the United States government. The government paid about 12 cents per acre.

All the Dakota bands were confined to a 150-mile long by 20-mile-wide reservation astride the Minnesota River—from west of Mankato to the western boundary of Minnesota. The U.S. government's payment to the tribes was to be spread over decades in the form of annuities. But the money was never adequate to cover expenses the Dakota incurred in transactions with government-authorized traders. Also, the annual payments were often late.

Because the Dakota bands no longer had access to the vast lands where they had hunted for generations, their survival soon came to depend on the promised government payments. The treaties' vague and at times contradictory terms, along with unkept promises and corrupt trading practices, brought misery and hunger to the Dakota people. Despite the attempts of some Dakota to adopt white farming practices, over years the situation worsened. Starvation became endemic and resentment grew, eventually leading to the tragedy of the U.S.-Dakota War of 1862. In that bloody conflict, hundreds of people were killed, both whites and Dakota. After the war, the Dakota were expelled altogether from the state of Minnesota.

When in 1870 Hinrich bought the Parcel A land in Wabasha County for $1,500, the Dakota had been gone for almost 20 years. The land he bought looked untouched and empty. But in fact, it had a rich and long history of human habitation. Whether Hinrich or anyone in his family was aware of that history is not known.

For further information, see *Confluence: A History of Fort Snelling*, by Hampton Smith. Minnesota Historical Society Press, St. Paul, 2021, and *The Story of Minnesota's Past*, by Rhoda R. Gilman. Minnesota Historical Society Press, St. Paul, 1989. See also the Minnesota Historical Society online, https://www.mnopedia.org/event/treaty-mendota-1851#

In his letter, Hinrich wrote that about one-third of the land had been broken and seeded that season, and that they had been able to harvest a modest crop. He estimated their net income at about $5.00/acre.[29] Now he encouraged Claus and Johann II to join the rest of the family in Minnesota, so they could buy more land.

The drive to obtain more land would become a refrain in subsequent letters. The family's history in Germany might help explain this. In Neuland Oste Dike, the family had owned a farm of no more than 20 acres, and there was no possibility of expansion. Johann I and Elisabeth had four sons and a daughter. It was not by accident but rather necessity that the three oldest sons all learned the carpentry trade. But farming was in their blood, and when they read about almost limitless land to buy and farm in America, they and thousands like them were enticed to emigrate. Indeed, the availability of land was like a magnet for hundreds of thousands of people—especially young men and including the Schlichtings of Neuland Oste Dike—drawing them to sell everything and leave for America.

Now the family had arrived in a place where they could realize their hopes for a new life in America. And they soon realized that even more land could be bought nearby. Despite the enormous energy required to break the virgin prairie sod,[30] that possibility must have seemed like a dream waiting to be fulfilled. In this letter, Hinrich urged his two younger brothers Claus and Johann II to leave their carpentry work in Milwaukee and to join the family on the new farm in Minnesota. There was no doubt in his mind. This part of his letter reads, "And you know which side of the matter Father is leaning toward. So later if you have any chance, come, entirely on your own (*ganz selbständig*), so we can buy a parcel of land."[31] Hinrich clearly wanted them to come to Minnesota; so did their father.

To illustrate how much they were needed, he ended the letter by writing that another two-thirds of the land (more than 100 acres) remained to be broken. The hint was obvious.

There is one more piece of information to gain from this letter. That Johann Jungclaus was working alongside Hinrich in this farming venture is revealed in a postscript Hinrich added. It raised the question of what should be done with the crops they had harvested that first season. Hinrich wrote, "Now we'll see if selling is the best, or transport, or railroad. It would be by horse and wagon. Johann [Jungclaus] will take care of the rest afterward." That singular comment makes it clear that the two cousins enjoyed a working relationship in this new enterprise.

---

[29] According to Hildegard Schmoelcke, this was the way German farmers at that time reckoned their harvests: using monetary value per land area (dollars per acre), as opposed to the yield in volume or weight per land area, for example, bushels per acre.

[30] John August Schlichting (1885-1968) could remember such labor. In *As I Remember*, p.7, he wrote that "the sod was broken with five horses hitched to a plow."

[31] The German text: *Ihr weist aber ja das [Vater] leich nach einer Seite fält wen ihr später gelegenheit hab zum Kommen so kommt ganz selbständig so das wir in Stück Land kaufen können* (reprinted exactly as Hinrich wrote it).

November 1870, Letter of Peter Schlichting, Breitenwisch, to Claus and Johann II, Milwaukee

The third letter from Peter in this group was written to Claus and Johann II in Milwaukee. It was not dated, but in the upper right corner Peter had scribbled a note: *the fortress of Metz has recently surrendered*. It is from this barely legible note that the letter can be dated to late October or early November 1870, shortly after the French surrendered the fortress during the Franco-Prussian War. Peter wrote that their cousin Hinrich (the son of his and Johann I's brother Diedrich) was serving in the Prussian army and was in or near Paris. Peter had begun the letter itself with the underlined word "Continuation" (*Fortsetzung*), followed by comments about help being given to several unfortunate people. The indication was that he had written earlier to his nephews about the situation. There was more neighborhood news, including word that Claus and Johann II's uncle, Anton Blank, was still living in their old farmhouse in Neuland Oste Dike and had rented some additional land. Finally, he added greetings from their grandfather Hinrich (Peter and Johann I's father), who was 85 years old, as well as from their two aunts Anna Margaretha and Metta (Peter and Johann I's sisters). The accompanying image is the first page of Peter's letter, with an arrow pointing to the comment about the fortress at Metz.

The first page of Peter's November 1870 letter bore no date, but the little note he later squeezed into the upper right-hand corner of the paper (arrow) made dating it possible. The note reads: "The fortress at Metz has recently surrendered," which places the letter in a timeframe of late October or early November 1870, during the Franco-Prussian war. The word Fortsetzung (Continuation), underlined and in the middle of the page, was the actual beginning of the letter.

Source: Schlichting Letters Collection: 1870-11 about-Peter S Brtnw to Claus Joh II S Mlwke

The Anton Blank Peter referred to was especially important in the early lives of our emigrant Schlichting family. Born in 1828, he was fourteen years younger than his sister Elisabeth, so

The Emigrant Letters ♦ 25

when Elisabeth married Johann I Schlichting in 1837, Anton was just nine years old. Johann and Elisabeth lived on the same Neuland farm—and in the same house—as Elisabeth's parents Claus and Ilse, and their youngest child Anton. Thus, Johann and Elisabeth's children were born into an extended family that included parents, grandparents, and their young uncle, Anton Blank.

When the last Schlichtings left Neuland for America in 1869, Anton, who by then was 41, remained in Neuland. He lived simply, and as Peter noted in his November 1870 letter, he continued to occupy their former farmhouse, at least for a while. Later, he worked at a nearby wind-powered watermill a few miles downstream along the Oste River. Eventually, he purchased land close to the mill and in 1880 built a small house just inside the dike. He kept a few sheep, engaged in commercial fishing on the river, and worked as a day laborer. When Peter Schlichting sent letters to the American family, he frequently included news about "Uncle Anton," knowing the close connection his niece and nephews had to their uncle.[32]

November 4, 1870, Letter of Peter Schlichting, Breitenwisch, to Johann I Schlichting, Minnesota

A final 1870 letter, dated November 4, is from Peter to his brother Johann I and his family. This, too, we have as an original, including the mailing envelope. It includes a great deal of news from the neighborhood, and it mentions briefly that Anton Blank, Johann I's brother-in-law, was doing well and had worked that summer on the construction of a new school in the village of Engelschoff, just east of Neuland. Peter wrote at some length about the Franco-Prussian war, celebrating Prussian victories and relating how his soldier nephew Hinrich—his and Johann I's brother Diedrich's son—had been involved when the fortress at Metz surrendered in late October. He wrote that the French fleet had bombarded the nearby seacoast and captured crews from Prussian ships: "From here we could hear the boom of the cannons firing at sea, and we were concerned that they might be paying us a visit along the coast."

The mailing envelope of Peter's Nov. 4, 1870, letter shows it was postmarked in the town of Hechthausen on Nov. 9. Note the unusual spelling of Lake City, which reflects Peter's attempt to write a name that, for him, was unusual. Why he wrote "via England" is uncertain.

Source: Schlichting Letters Collection: 1870-11-04 Peter S Brtnw to Joh I MN

---

[32] I have written an essay about Anton titled "Anton Blank, A Favorite Uncle" and am happy to provide a copy upon request.

The crop harvest and livestock reports were positive, including a good harvest of honey from his bees. Finally, he made a request for news from America, seeing as "It's been a long time since your last letter." He ended once again with greetings from his father Hinrich and from his sisters Anna Margaretha and Metta.

CHAPTER 3
LETTERS FROM 1871
Sorrow and Loss

Date	Source	Writer in Germany / Recipient	Writer in U.S. / Recipient	Comments
1871, poss. 1870	original		probably Claus Schlichting, Milwaukee, to the family in Minn.	Johann II had been ill, needed medicine. He tried to work when able but was preoccupied by the family not being there.
1871	prov. by Hildegard Schmoelcke		Johann Jungclaus, Lake City, Minn., to an unknown recipient in Germany	Johann J. had received the person's letter before Christmas; Johann's letters weren't being answered. He was faring well, as were the Schlichtings.
mid-1871, Johann Jungclaus left the Minnesota farm and returned to Neuland Oste Dike, Germany.				
1871, July	original		Anton Schlichting, Lake City, Minn., to his brothers Claus & Johann II, Milwaukee.	They had broken the other 80 acres. Entire 160 acres now fenced. Granary built. Potato bug problems. He just turned 17. They had received letter from Uncle Peter in Germany that their Aunt Metta had married.
1871 September 16, Anton Schlichting, youngest son of Johann I & Elisabeth Schlichting, became sick and died at age 17, on the farm in Wabasha County, Minnesota.				
1871, late September	original		Hinrich S, Lake City, Minn., to Claus & Joh. II S, Mlwke.	Anton had become ill and had died; father Johann I greatly distressed, also dissatisfied with life in America and wished he were back in Germany.
1871, Oct. 31/Nov. 1	original		Johann I S, Lake City, Minn., to Claus & Joh II S, Mlwke.	He wanted his sons to come to Minn. and buy land; he was unhappy with their reluctance to come. Their aunt in Germany, Metta, had married. He recounted the last days with Anton, and Anton's death & burial.
1871, Nov. 6	photocopy		Hinrich S, Lake City, Minn., to Claus & Joh II S, Mlwke.	Urged the brothers not to rush to get to Minn., and to bring all their things. Joh. Jungclaus had left for Germany. Hinrich had given him $500. Their father was somewhat better.
1871, Nov. 14	original		Johann I, Lake City, Minn., to Claus & Joh II S, Mlwke.	Was very pleased C&J were coming to Minn. & glad they weren't going to Chicago.
1871 Dec., Claus and Johann II left Milwaukee and joined the rest of the family in Wabasha County, Minnesota.				

The Emigrant Letters ♦ 29

The year 1871 brought significant changes to the Schlichtings in Minnesota, including tragedy and the grieving that followed it. The chart above lists the letters in our collection from that year. Noticeably lacking are any letters from Peter Schlichting in Germany. He certainly wrote (see Anton's letter from July), but the letters have been lost. The next letter in the collection from Peter is from March 1873.

1870 or 1871 Note from Claus Schlichting, Milwaukee, to family in Minnesota

The first of the letters is a brief, undated and unsigned note written from Milwaukee by Claus Schlichting. Although his name is missing, the handwriting matches that in letters he wrote and signed. It stated that his brother, Johann II, had been ill and needed medicine, but that he was working whenever he could. Claus added a wistful comment: "[Johann] is preoccupied with many thoughts, especially that you are not here."

The note presents problems, including that it was scribbled on the back of an envelope and stuffed into another envelope with a different letter. That other letter has been lost. An exact date cannot be determined, but the time must have been late 1870 or early 1871, when Claus and Johann II were still in Milwaukee. The structure of the note is jumbled and grammatically confusing, making translation a challenge.

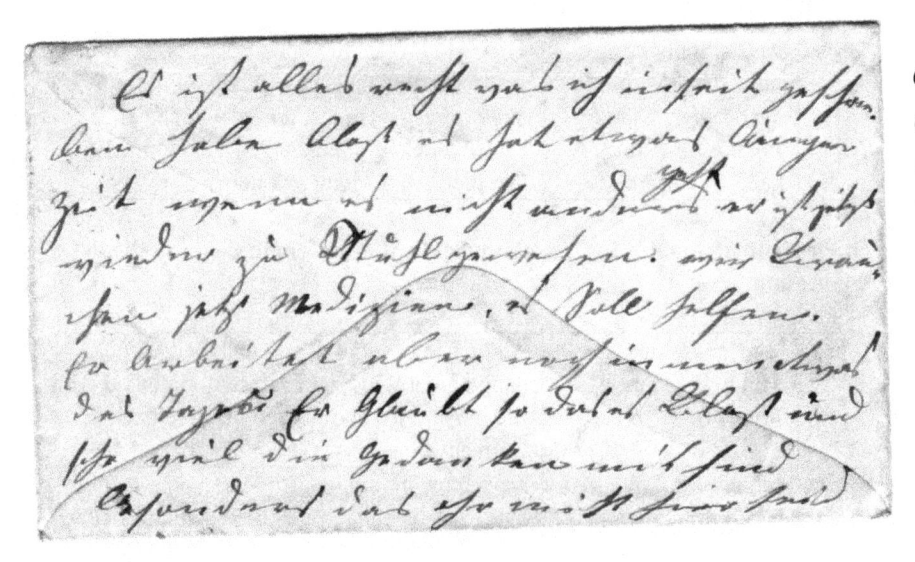

Claus' enigmatic note on the back of an envelope regarding his brother's illness. It ends wistfully with, "[Johann] is preoccupied with many thoughts, especially that you are not here."

Source: Schlichting Letters Collection: 1871 about Claus S Mlwke to Family MN

1871 Letter of Johann Jungclaus, Minnesota, to an unnamed recipient in Germany

The next letter in the group was mentioned in Chapter 2. It was written by Johann Jungclaus from Lake City, Minn. Though undated, its contents, together with a comment by Hinrich S. in a letter he wrote on November 6, indicate that it was written in early to mid-1871. Its importance for our purposes lies in Johann Jungclaus' comment that both he and the Schlichtings were faring well. This indicates that he was either living with them or close by. Hinrich's Nov. 6 letter points to the former. The significance of Johann Jungclaus for the Schlichting family in Minnesota will be discussed further.

July 1871, Letter of Anton Schlichting, Minnesota, to his brothers
Claus and Johann II, Milwaukee

This is the only surviving letter written by Anton, the youngest of the Schlichting brothers. He wrote it to his brothers in Milwaukee on July 14, the day after his 17th birthday. He reported progress in breaking new land and completing the fencing of their 160-acre farm (Parcel A), along with the building of a granary.[33] Potato beetles were a problem that summer. The family had received a letter from Peter Schlichting in Germany, informing them of the marriage of Anton's aunt, Metta, to Johann Andreas Hellwege earlier that year.[34] What makes his letter bittersweet is the knowledge that within two months, Anton, happy to have turned 17 in July, would become ill, and would die on September 16.

September 1871, Letter of Hinrich Schlichting, Minnesota, to brothers
Claus and Johann II, Milwaukee

Anton's July letter leads to a letter written by oldest brother Hinrich, in September, to his two brothers in Milwaukee. In it he informed Claus and Johann II of Anton's illness and death on September 16 at the age of 17. Their sister Rebecka (18) had had the same illness—possibly typhoid fever—but it was not as severe. A letter from Claus and Johann II had arrived just days before Anton died, so he had been able to hear their greeting. What Hinrich then added in this letter reflected the grief affecting the three remaining family members. His own grieving aside, Hinrich was concerned by his father's deep distress, which expressed itself in bitter complaints about life in America, and in rebukes directed at his sons—especially Hinrich—for the way they were "help[ing] themselves to all his assets." Hinrich wrote that their father wanted the family to be together again, but he also began voicing a wish to go back to Germany. Hinrich's own frustration spilled over into this letter: "As you have seen from his letters, Father is very dissatisfied. If God would grant it, I would wish with all my heart that Father and his money were back in Germany—so I could finally have peace again ... Father berates this country (*wie Vater über dieses Land schimpft*) ... Even on the day of [Anton's] funeral, he told me, in that old way of his, that he could just as well go back to his village."[35] These uncharacteristically sharp comments reveal the fraught state of emotions among the three surviving family members.[36]

---

[33] This land had been purchased by Hinrich S. in June of 1870. It is referred to as "Parcel A" because it was the first land the family owned in Minnesota. Its location near Jacksonville, Minn. is described and shown in *Hinrich*, pp. 84-86.
[34] Metta was the youngest sister of Anton's father Johann I. She and Johann Andreas Hellwege married on May 21 and settled in the village of Kleinwoerden, just across the Oste River from Neuland. Her name was sometimes spelled "Mette."
[35] 1871-09-abt Hinrich S MN to Claus Joh II S Mlwke.
[36] Johann I's homesickness did not go away. Finally, in June 1876, his four living children signed an affidavit that pledged their financial support for him, should he decide to return to and remain in Germany. This will be dealt with in Chapter 5. See also *Hinrich*, p.110.

Oct. 31/Nov. 1, 1871, Letter of Johann I in Minnesota to his sons Claus and Johann II in Milwaukee

On October 31/November 1, Johann I wrote his own letter to his sons Claus and Johann II, in which he openly vented his grief and distress. He chided his sons for failing to come to Minnesota, where they could easily have purchased land and at good prices. But now the land was being bought up quickly; they were missing their chance. He recalled how they had only reluctantly left Germany, while Hinrich had done so "of his own free will." He used a few quaint sayings to express urgency, writing that they should "do [their] duty" and come. Then he added, "I have loved my children more than father, brothers, sisters, or fatherland. But who knows what lies before me. As the saying goes, 'The cart is waiting outside my door.'"

Yet despite his anguish, Johann I's deep faith still rose to the surface. He closed the letter by writing, "My sick son Anton and I received Holy Communion together and in faith for the forgiveness of sins. I was present with a community for the funeral of my son. I also was at the church, the funeral service. And I was at my son's final resting place, the committal service. In the name of the Father, and of the Son, and of the Holy Spirit. Amen. —Johann Schlichting, the 1st of November 1871

"The Holy Bible is filled with inexpressibly lofty meaning, but the best word in it is, 'Peace with God and with man.' That was the song of the angels at Jesus' birth."

Anton's body was laid to rest at a rural cemetery in West Albany Township in Wabasha County. Four years later, on November 20, 1875, Hinrich set a gravestone at the site. The stone is still there.[37]

Johann II made the following notation and sketch in his journal page for 1875:
"20 Nov H[inrich] set Anton's gravestone."
Source: Johann II Schlichting Journal Part 3, p. 23

Nov. 6, 1871, Letter of Hinrich S, Minnesota, to his brothers Claus and Johann II, Milwaukee

Less than a week after Johann I sent the above letter, Hinrich also wrote his brothers. From this November 6 letter we can ascertain that Claus and Johann II had already indicated their intention to join the family in Minnesota. Hinrich encouraged this, partly for his, his father's, and sister's sakes, but also because he needed them.

---

[37] Johann Schlichting II Journal, Part 3, p. 23. Also noted in his chronological chart on p. 33. A photo of the grave marker can be found in *Hinrich*, p. 87.

Merlin Schlichting ♦ 32

Hinrich's spare writing style is apparent in this Nov. 6, 1871, letter to his brothers in Milwaukee. By then, he was aware that Claus and Johann II would be coming to Minnesota. He noted (top arrow): "Jo[hann] Jungclaus has returned to Germany with 500 d[ollars]. Perhaps he will return." He also assured them that their father's distress had eased somewhat (lower arrow): "Father's anguish has eased a little. It's like the old saying, 'After the storm the weather is good.'"

Source: Schlichting Letters Collection: 1871-11-06 Hinrich S MN to Claus Joh II S Mlwke

As noted in the caption to the image above, it is in this letter that he wrote about Johann Jungclaus' departure earlier in the year. This cousin had lived with the Schlichtings for more than a year and had provided invaluable help as they broke the prairie soil and began to farm the 160 acres Hinrich had bought in June of 1870. But after learning of his own father's unexpected death in April in Neuland, Johann Jungclaus decided to return to Germany.[38] Most likely he left in late spring or early summer. The Schlichtings sent him on his way with $500, a sizable sum of money.

Johann Jungclaus had labored alongside his cousin Hinrich, breaking land, building fences, constructing buildings, and doing other needed tasks. He was sorely missed. With his departure, and after Anton's death, only Hinrich (34), his father Johann (61), and sister Rebecka (18) remained to tend their new farm.

But despite Hinrich's desire to have his brothers come and join the family in Minnesota, he cautioned them not to rush leaving Milwaukee, and not to "throw away any of your things," by which he probably meant carpentry tools. He also wrote, "Remember that you left Germany in too much of a hurry, and that always has disadvantages."

---

[38] Johann J's father Diedrich died April 25, 1871, at age 61.

The Emigrant Letters • 33

November 14, 1871, Letter of Johann I, Minnesota, to his sons Claus and Johann II, Milwaukee

While Anton's death had shaken the whole family, in early October another momentous event occurred: the great Chicago fire that destroyed much of that city.[39] In his journal, Johann II wrote that he and Claus had contemplated moving there because carpenters would be needed for rebuilding.[40] They must have written as much to the Minnesota family, though such a letter is not in our collection. Receiving that news, however, might have been behind some of what their father Johann I wrote back to them in his letter of October 31/November 1, in particular his comment, "Maybe it's better in bigger cities, and perhaps now again in Chicago."

In that same letter, Johann I had argued for their joining the rest of the family in Minnesota, using as motivation the case for buying land before it got too expensive. And as noted above, he reprimanded them for failing to join the family there, perhaps intended as further motivation.

Sometime after receiving their father's pointed letter, Claus and Johann II made the decision to go to Minnesota—not Chicago—and had written as much to the family there. That letter is not in our collection but must have been written.

Upon receiving that news, their father Johann I promptly wrote this letter of November 14. He began it by writing, "That you are coming to us here is dear to me. God will show us what we have yet to do and to let go in Minnesota." He advised them, "Close out your affairs in Milwaukee in an orderly and honorable manner, to whatever extent possible. For the trip here pay whatever you must." He also wrote that he truly had not wanted them to go to Chicago. As he put it, "... [Chicago] soon will be overfilled, and ... [it] is half as bad as Sodom and Gomorrah."[41] He ended the letter by stating his firm conviction that God would continue to bless them all.

Hinrich added a postscript, writing that while it would be good if they could pay for their own travel, "... if you need money, write in good time, not in a big hurry—good order, good prayer."[42]

The decision to leave Milwaukee and to venture west to the Minnesota farm was not an easy one for Claus and Johann II. In his journal, Johann II had noted all the jobs they had taken on during their three-and-a-half years in Milwaukee. It was a considerable number.[43] On the other hand, the year 1871 was ending with financial losses. Johann II summarized their debts in his journal:

Money from Cincinnati, May 1868, both	$550
Sent to Minnesota in '71:	
to Hinrich	$300
to father	200
our expenses	400
	$900 debt
In a span of 3½ years a loss for both,	$1,450.[44]

---

[39] The fire took place October 8-10, 1871.
[40] Johann Schlichting II, op. cit, p. 19.
[41] This was a reference to the biblical cities of those names mentioned in the book of Genesis, starting in Chapter 10. They were identified as wicked places, filled with vice and immorality.
[42] The handwriting in the postscript is Hinrich's, as opposed to the handwriting in the body of the letter, which matches his father's.
[43] Johann II Schlichting, op. cit., pp. 14-19.
[44] Johann II Schlichting, op. cit., p. 19.

$1,450 was a lot of money in 1871, and given their setbacks, it is not hard to understand the attraction Chicago held for Claus and Johann II. After the devastation of the fire, carpenters would no doubt be in high demand, and the brothers presumably would have a chance to make good on their losses. But their younger brother's death in September, together with a realization of the heavy responsibility their older brother Hinrich now bore as sole provider and laborer on the Minnesota farm, ultimately drew them to their family.

Johann II noted in his journal that the last weeks he and Claus spent in Milwaukee were hard: "Toward the end [of our time in Milwaukee], life was very difficult. We went to the theater several times, just to lift our spirits a little and to avoid depressing thoughts."[45] It was a hard time for the family all around.

Johann II left Milwaukee on December 13, with Claus following on the 22nd. Johann wrote that by Christmas they were with their father, Rebecka, and Hinrich in Minnesota.[46] The year 1872 would see the reunited family undertaking new tasks and solidifying their farming enterprise in Minnesota.

---

[45] Ibid. That this comment was omitted from the translation in *New World Beginnings*, p. 33, is unfortunate.

[46] Ibid.

CHAPTER 4
1873-1875

Productive Years in Minnesota, Hard Years in the Old Country

Date	Source	Writer - Recipient	Comments
1873 Mar. 31	original	Peter Schlichting, Breitenwisch, to Johann I Schlichting & Family, Minn.	Peter & Johann I's father Hinrich (1785-1874) was frail. Their sister Anna Margaretha also not well. Crops & livestock reports. Sister Metta & husband had a daughter. Peter had lost eels & beehives to theft. Prices generally higher. Noted a letter received from Johann I.
1873 Dec. 17	original	Peter S, Brtnw, to Johann I S, Minn.	Father Hinrich's condition deteriorating. Brother Diedrich working at Kuhla estate but not well. Acknowledged receipt of money from Johann I. Neighborhood news and crop report. Wrote about a scandal reg. a neighbor, Peter K. Infrastructure: Nov. storm overflowed dike. New locks nearly complete.
1874 Jan. 11	photocopy	Diedrich S, Brtnw, to Johann I S, Minn.	Earliest letter of Diedrich in the PDX collection. He thanked Johann I for gift of money. Couldn't work due to shortness of breath. Wrote about his three children.
1874 Jan. 17, "Grandfather" Hinrich Schlichting died, in Breitenwisch, Germany, aged 88 (father of Johann I, Diedrich, Anna Margaretha, Peter, and Metta).			
1874 Feb. 18	original	Peter S, Brtnw, to Johann I S, Minn.	Neighborhood news and infrastructure report. Mild winter. Peter's wife Margrethe was ill.
1874 Apr. 12	original	Peter S, Brtnw, to Johann I S, Minn.	March storms caused damage. Neighborhood news: many people sick with edema. Peter's wife very sick. Thanked for money sent.
1874 May 13	original	Peter S, Brtnw, to Johann I S, Minn.	Wife very ill, edema and sores. Diedrich was helping in kitchen but had trouble breathing. Neighborhood news included a suicide. Reported about roads built. Sister Anna Marg. not well. Thanked for money sent.
1874 May about	photocopy	Diedrich S, Brtnw, to Johann I S, Minn.	Repeated much of Jan. 11 letter. Thanked again for money sent and stated the amount.
1874 May about	photocopy	Peter S, Brtnw, to Johann I S, Minn.	He reported neighborhood news on the back of Diedrich's letter.
1874 June 30	original	Peter S, Brtnw, to Johann I S, Minn.	Wife's condition worse. Weather dry & cold, had to replant potatoes. Scandal re. Peter K.: he had attacked pastor and had impregnated a young girl. Explained about new Prussian marriage law.
1874 July 21	original	Peter & Diedrich S, Brtnw, to Johann I S, Minn.	Wife's condition unchanged. Peter was concerned for his bees. Drought. He took some bee hives to Anton Blank. Peter K. committed to an institution. Thanked for money sent. Diedrich added some comments.

1874 Oct. 14	original	Peter S, Brtnw, to Johann I S, Minn.	Peter was caring for wife with Diedrich's help. Crops & livestock: potatoes dug, poor quality; low honey production due to bad weather in August. Local teacher Sommer elected to be marriage registrar for Horst.

1874 Oct. 22, Margrethe Schlichting died, in Breitenwisch, aged 36 (Peter Schlichting's first wife).

1874 Nov. 10	original	Peter S, Brtnw, to Johann I S, Minn.	Peter wrote of his wife Margrethe's death on Oct. 22. Strong storm and flood same day. His sister Metta & family in Kleinwoerden were flooded out. Peter helped clean up house. Crop and livestock prices were low.
1874 Dec. 13	photocopy	Peter S, Brtnw, to Johann I S, Minn.	Diedrich was very ill; Peter was caring for him. He reflected on his marriage and current situation. He reported flood damage: dike breach repaired; relief efforts underway for those affected.
1874 Dec. 13	photocopy	Prof. A. Craemer, St. Louis MO, to Hinrich S, Minn.	A letter from Prof. Craemer regarding an inquiry Hinrich had made about entering seminary.
1875 Jan. 12	photocopy	Peter S, Brtnw, to Johann I S, Minn.	Diedrich was somewhat improved. Their sister Anna M. had gone to live with sister Metta in Kleinwoerden. Anton Blank visited at Christmas. Neighborhood news. Reported on assessments for infrastructure projects.
1875 Jan .20	photocopy	Prof. A. Craemer, St. Louis MO, to Hinrich S, Minn.	Follow-up to his letter of Dec. 13.
1875 Mar. 13	original	Peter S, Brtnw, to Johann I S, Minn.	Wrote an update on the Peter K. saga. Reported changes to monetary & military systems. He had served as witness to a marriage. Neighborhood news.
1875 Nov. 8	original	Peter S, Brtnw, to Johann I S, Minn.	Peter and Johann I's sister Anna Margaretha had died Nov. 2. Wrote about his bees and about repair work on their house. New school built in Neuland. He asked for a letter, had received none for a long time.

Before starting the discussion about this group of letters, it is important to recapitulate events for the Schlichtings in America, starting in 1870.

In June of 1870, Hinrich and his father Johann I bought their first property in America: 160 acres of land in Gillford Township, Wabasha County, Minnesota. In the book *Hinrich* it is referred to as Parcel A. This was unbroken prairie grassland. Little is known of the family's living conditions in their first years on that land, including what kind of house they built or how their animals were sheltered. Members of the family that fall were Johann I (age 60), daughter Rebecka (17), and sons Hinrich (33) and Anton (16). In spring or early summer 1870 they were joined by their cousin Johann Jungclaus (28), who had come to America in 1869 on the same ship as the Schlichtings. He lived and worked with them.[47]

In an October 3, 1870, letter to his brothers Claus and Johann II in Milwaukee, Hinrich indicated that they—meaning himself, Johann Jungclaus, Anton, and perhaps Johann I—had "broken;" that is to say, plowed, a third of the virgin land—roughly 55 acres—and had sown and harvested a modest crop.[48]

In mid-1871, Johann Jungclaus left and returned to Germany.[49] Then in September Anton became sick and died. This left only Johann I (by then 61), Hinrich (34) and Rebecka (18) on the farm. Claus (31) and Johann II (27) arrived from Milwaukee late in December 1871, as discussed in Chapter 3.

Sometime after he and Claus had arrived, Johann II constructed a tabular chart as part of his journal. The chart provided information about the farm: crop yields, purchase of work animals, digging of wells, building a house, etc., along with numerous sketches in the margins. The chart begins in December 1871 with his and Claus' arrival from Milwaukee, with subsequent entries following chronologically.[50]

---

[47] For an extensive discussion of the family's early years in Minnesota, see *Hinrich*, Chapter 6, and Chapter 7 pp. 93ff. Johann Jungclaus' close association with the Schlichtings is evidenced by several references in letters and in Johann II's journal. At the time research was being done for the *Hinrich* book, however, little was known about him, because his presence with the family in Minnesota more than a hundred years earlier had been forgotten. Beyond that, his surname was misread as "Jungoldus" in the first translation of Johann II's journal (see *New World Beginnings*, p. 31). Ancestry.com researchers made the same mistake when reading the ship manifest (see *Hinrich*, p. 60). Finally, his actual blood relationship to the Schlichtings had long since been forgotten (he was a second cousin to Johann I and Elisabeth Schlichting's children).

[48] As David Schlichting described in *Hinrich*, the "breaking" of virgin prairie soil was arduous work and required both man- and horsepower. See *Hinrich*, pp. 85-86.

[49] Johann Jungclaus' father Diedrich died on April 24, 1871, at 61 years of age. When Johann learned of this, he left Minnesota—probably late spring or early summer—and returned to Neuland. He later married and raised a family there.

[50] Johann II Schlichting Journal, Part 3, p. 31. In the upper left corner of the chart Johann wrote, "We arrive, December 1871" (*wir kommen 71 Decemb.*).

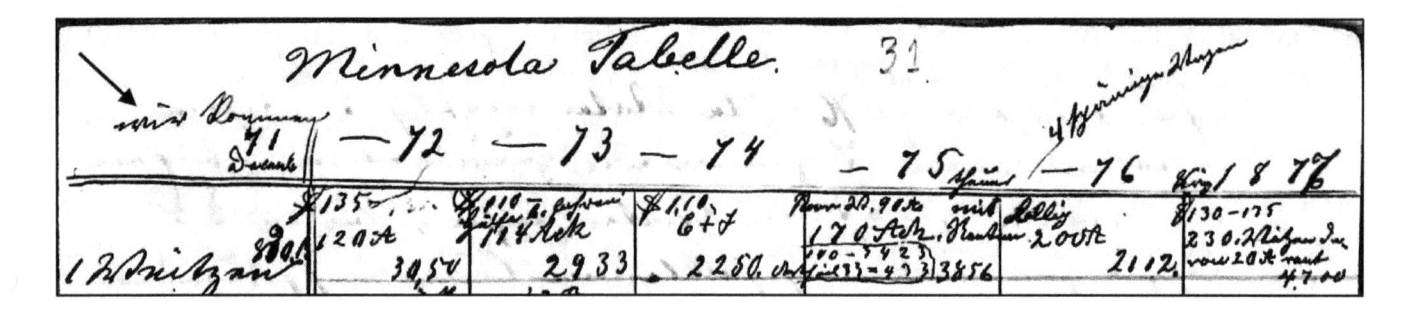

The top line of Johann II's Minnesota Tabelle begins with his and Claus' arrival in Minnesota (arrow): "We arrive 71 Decemb" (wir kommen 71 Decemb).
   Source: Johann II Schlichting Journal Part 3, p. 31

There are no letters in the collection from 1872. All the letters in the chart above arrived during a three-year period from 1873 through 1875. Nearly all of them were written by Johann I's brother Peter in Germany.[51] A few were written by another brother, Diedrich,[52] who by then was widowed and living with Peter and his wife Margrethe on the Schlichting farm in Breitenwisch.

What we can learn of the Schlichtings in Minnesota during those years must be gleaned from Johann II's journal, along with deeds for land purchased, plat maps, and the like. A great deal of information is documented in *Hinrich* in chapters 6 and 7. But the letters from Germany between 1873 and 1875 also give us insights into communication between the families on the two sides of the Atlantic. For example, on several occasions in these three years, the Americans had sent money to their German relatives. Receipt of the money was acknowledged in letters sent by Peter or Diedrich to their brother Johann I in America.

---

[51] Peter Schlichting (1833-1894) was Johann I's youngest brother.
[52] Diedrich (also spelled Diederich) Schlichting (1815-1883), was Johann I's next younger brother.

Merlin Schlichting ♦ 40

1872-1874: Productive Years on the Minnesota Farm

The first words Johann II wrote in his journal for 1872 were, "Arriving in Minnesota, we were struck by its remoteness."[53] This was Claus and Johann II's first exposure to the open expanse of the Minnesota prairie. Having spent the past several years in a city environment, it no doubt took them some time to adjust. But the long winter—they arrived in December—also gave them opportunity to address urgent needs. Johann wrote that in those cold months they "...did some work on the house, along with some carpentry. The main job, however, was to dig a 62-foot deep well. Before that, Hinrich had been hauling water on a sled, and for a while we melted snow." [54]

He continued, "We had two horses and two milk cows [Johann added a sketch of a horse in the margin]. We bought a third [cow] from Lefsen [sic],[55] a yearling steer, and one heifer, all kept in a straw barn. In spring we bought two more horses for $336 [in the margin Johann drew a sketch of two more horses]."

First Hinrich and then Johann II used two horses to help their immediate neighbor to the east, named Wempner, break 80 acres of land. Johann II wrote about a successful harvest of wheat, oats, barley, corn, and potatoes, and he named several neighbors who helped them with the grain harvest. The family purchased a wagon for $95 (another sketch in the margin), and a second plow, which he also sketched.

---

[53] Johann II Schlichting, op. cit. p. 20. Johann's German text: *Als wir in Minnesota angekommen waren kamm es uns erst recht einsam vor*.
[54] Johann II Schlichting op. cit., p. 20.
[55] According to an 1877 plat map, this neighbor's name was John Lafson. He owned the quarter-section just across from the Schlichtings along what is now County Road 31. See *Hinrich*, p. 96.

Johann often drew sketches of what he wrote about in his journal. In this page for the year 1872, he sketched: 1) a 62-foot well they dug, 2) a one-year-old ox they purchased, 3) two horses they bought for $336, and 4) below, a wagon they bought for $95.

Source: Johann II Schlichting Journal Part 3, p. 20

On the page describing farm work in the following year, 1873, Johann II wrote that a second well had been dug to 40 feet, "where we first struck a good flow of water."[56] They built a horse barn with a straw roof, and in spring they bought a used threshing machine for $615, along with two hinnies to use as work animals.[57] Another new wagon was bought. Johann sketched all of them in the margin.

Johann II's report for 1874 was equally positive.[58] It included the purchase of an additional 40 acres of land from a neighbor he identified as Mack.[59] Johann drew a sketch of the acreage in the margin. Several neighbors who helped with the grain harvest were named; some had helped in previous years. Johann's unique way of identifying them makes for entertaining reading. Equally important, it reflected a considerable ethnic mix in the neighborhood. Johann wrote, "At harvest time our helpers were: 1. Frank Schulmeister, 2. his friend, 3. Dan from '73, 4. old Blehm, 5. (from '72) the small Dutchman,[60] 6. the Swede, 7. old Hinrich ('73) for stacking, 8. Red Johann, 8 [sic]. his countryman, 9. [illegible] Hinrich, 10. a Pomeranian, 11. a High German, 12. an Irishman."[61] A third plow was purchased, a sketch of which Johann added in the margin. He wrote further that they slaughtered nine hogs and one beef animal. During fall they "rolled away" the straw barn and added 38 feet of new structure to the barn.

An underscored *N[ota] bene* ("Note well" or "Note especially") was added. On September 6 a new pastor had begun serving the Lutheran congregation in West Albany. On November 1 four members of the Schlichting family received Holy Communion.[62]

All these journal entries point to a family that had settled into its new community and had good relations with neighbors. The virgin prairie they turned into farmland proved very productive. In short, they were faring well, both as a family and economically. The last is certainly a reason they were able to send money to the relatives back in Germany.

---

[56] Johann II Schlichting, op. cit., p. 21.
[57] A hinny (in German, *Maulesel*) is the offspring of a female donkey and a male horse, as opposed to a mule (in German, *Maultier*), which is the offspring of a male donkey and a female horse.
[58] Johann II Schlichting, op. cit., p. 22.
[59] "Mack" referred to James McIntosh. Johann sometimes wrote "Maik."
[60] "Dutchman," Johann wrote *Holänder* (a misspelling of *Holländer*).
[61] *Ibid.* Thirteen men were identified (Johann used the number 8 twice). The first name of No. 9 is not clearly legible.

[62] At that time, the Schlichtings were still affiliated with the Lutheran congregation in West Albany Township. In the Lutheran tradition, the sacraments (Holy Baptism and Holy Communion) could only be administered by an ordained pastor. The pastor who served the West Albany congregation served other congregations as well, following the "circuit rider" pattern for frontier areas. Thus, on many Sundays no pastor was present, so worship gatherings were led by laymen. Worship on such Sundays would consist of Scripture readings, hymns, prayers, and often the reading of a sermon from a collection of published sermons. The sacraments would be administered only when the pastor was present.

Letters from Germany, 1873-1875

As the Schlichtings in Minnesota worked to establish and secure their farming endeavor, their relatives in Germany continued to send news of what was happening there. As stated above, there are no letters in our collection from 1872, but there are several from 1873, 1874, and 1875, all from Germany to the American family. Important or repeated themes in the various letters include:

- The fragile condition of Grandfather Hinrich (1785-1874). He was the father of Johann I, Diedrich, Anna Margaretha,[63] Peter, and Metta.
- Money received from the American family, mentioned in several letters.
- Brother Diedrich's intermittent poor health, mostly respiratory in nature.
- Two letters by Diedrich, which included news of his three children, Hinrich, Johann, and Anna.
- Beginning in February 1874, descriptions of the illness and progressive decline of Peter's wife Margrethe ("Gretchen"), the nursing care given her by Peter and Diedrich, and her death on October 22, 1874.
- Inclement weather, especially in 1874, resulting in poor crops and low honey production.
- Changes in Prussian laws regarding marriage, monetary reform, and restructuring of the military.
- The death on Nov. 2, 1875, of Anna Margaretha Schlichting, Johann I, Diedrich, Peter, and Metta's sister.
- Road construction projects, and the enlarging of the Burgbeck Canal and its financing.

---

[63] In his letters, Peter spelled his sister Anna Margaretha's name in various ways. For this work, I use the name that was stated in her baptismal record entry: Anna Margaretha.

In this sequence of letters, Peter was writing roughly once a month. In six separate letters we read that the Americans had sent money on at least five occasions. In one letter, Peter wrote, "God bless you and your children for the repeated good deeds done for us. Saying thank you seems too weak on my part, but by God's grace it's as though you knew just how I am faring."[64] The actual amount sent was named in two letters (from December 1873 and from May 1874), given in the currency of Breitenwisch at the time: thaler (pronounced *TAH-ler*), silver coins (*Groschen*), and pennies (*Pfennig*). That Johann I and his family continued to support those they had left behind is certainly a testament to their loyalty. But it is also a witness—evidenced by comments like the one above—to their German relatives' financial need. During these years when the American family was establishing itself in southeastern Minnesota, the gifts of money indicate that the family's financial situation was at least stable.

In a letter of March 31, 1873,[64] Peter wrote about the deteriorating health of his father Hinrich Schlichting (1785-1874). As noted above, Hinrich was the father of Johann I, Diedrich, Anna Margaretha, Peter, and Metta,[65] and was still living on the Breitenwisch farm. He was 88, an extraordinary age for that time. Peter and his wife Margrethe cared for him. Through the winter, Peter's brother Diedrich, who lived with them on the farm, also had been ill with a chronic respiratory condition.

In December, Peter wrote that his father's health continued to decline: "Father's condition is just this: he cannot help himself."[66] That translated into around-the-clock care for him by Peter and Margrethe. Diedrich had recovered enough to work through the summer, but with the onset of cold weather, his respiratory difficulties had returned. In the same letter, Peter also acknowledged a gift of money from America: "We received the money you sent, delivered by the postman here to the house. It amounted to 32 thaler, 6 silver coins, and 8 pennies. We all thank you. In good time it will be carefully spent."

Grandfather Hinrich died January 17, 1874. Soon after that, Peter's wife Margrethe began to suffer from a debilitating and progressive illness. Each subsequent letter Peter wrote that year described her worsening condition and the care he—and Diedrich as he was able—gave her. She died on October 22. Diedrich still was not well. In addition to all of that, on the day of Margrethe's death a terrific storm blew in from the North Sea, resulting in flooding and causing dikes to fail. Peter's sister Metta and her family were flooded out of their house in Kleinwoerden. All this weighed heavily on Peter. In a December 13, 1874, letter he wrote, "I am barely returned from my wife's grave and find myself burdened yet again by illness...It is night and I am writing at my brother's bedside. The bleakness brings tears to my eyes. I will care for Diedrich as well as I can. Metta and Anna Magretha [sic] have left, so I am here alone."[67] Thankfully, by January of 1875, Peter could write that Diedrich's health had improved.

---

[64] 1873-03-31 Peter S Brtnw to Joh I S MN.
[65] Metta's name was sometimes spelled "Mette."
[66] "1873-12-17 Peter S Brtnw to Johann I S MN"
[67] Anna Margaretha was living with her sister Metta and husband at their farm in Kleinwoerden, a village two to three miles from Breitenwisch, on the opposite bank of the Oste River.

The Lutheran church in Horst, viewed here from the south, was built between 1150 and 1250. The church was built on a sandy rise—called "The Horst"—surrounded by low-lying moorland and close to the Oste River. In early years it also would have served as a haven during times of flooding. It was the parish church of our ancestral Schlichting family. Although their grave markers are no longer present, Grandfather Hinrich Schlichting (1785-1874) and Peter Schlichting's wife Margrethe (1838-1874) would have been buried in this cemetery adjacent to the church building. That cemetery was closed in 1885, and a new cemetery was opened farther to the south.

Diedrich's three children, Hinrich, Johann, and Anna, were mentioned several times. Of interest is that one son, Johann, emigrated to America in 1883 and settled near St. Paul, Minnesota. Twelve years later, in 1895, he sent two letters to his cousins Claus and Hinrich in Oregon. (Hinrich and his family had arrived there from Minnesota the previous October.) Either Hinrich or Claus must have written first, since Johann's first letter was a response. Johann's letters appeared in translation in *New World Beginnings* on p. 13. They will be discussed in another chapter.

Peter's letters were newsy; that is, he filled them with the latest information about people and places his American relatives knew, frequently including news about Uncle Anton Blank. He frequently wrote about crops planted and how they fared, prices both for purchasing and for selling, and about weather. Peter kept hives of bees and transported them to various locations as seasons and weather changed. In a later letter (March 1877), he wrote that one of his winter chores—and means of earning income—was weaving beehives, likely from willow branches.

"News" sometimes included unique stories about individuals. One that was more notable involved a man named Peter Kuehlke. Peter Schlichting wrote about him over the course of several months, beginning in June 1874. Kuehlke, who from Peter's description was a chronic alcoholic, had managed to get the key to the church in Grossenwoerden and in a drunken state had gone in, torn the altar cloth from the altar and flung it over the pulpit. The next Sunday he grabbed the pastor by the throat and threatened him. The man had also impregnated a young girl working at his farm—the third time he had done such a thing. Peter wrote that Kuehlke was being closely watched (*bewacht*) by the authorities. In July, Peter wrote that Kuehlke had been taken to a mental institution, and the following March wrote that he had been transferred to another, more distant, institution. Such a story is witness not only to the fact that societal crises happened then as well as now, but also that the resources available to deal with them, especially in a small rural community, were limited and that protection for the innocent was often lacking. It was a situation that, sadly, can just as well be true today.

Weather is a favorite topic for all farmers, and Peter wrote about it in most of his letters. The year 1874 seems to have had more than its share of adverse weather, from a late spring frost to summer drought to fall storms. He had to replant his potatoes because of the late frost, and the same frost killed most of the barley sprouts. During August, abnormally cool weather hindered the blooming of many wildflowers, which resulted in a poor harvest of honey. Finally, on October 22, as noted above, a major storm caused damage and flooding, forcing Peter's sister Metta and her family in Kleinwoerden to evacuate their house, which Peter then helped repair.

Societal structure was changing during these years. The German Empire had been established in 1871 under the authority of the Prussian government and king (now called emperor, *Kaiser*). Peter wrote in June 1874, then again in March 1875, about three notable changes:

- The requirement that legal marriage ceremonies would now take place in a registrar's office rather than in a church. To that end, a civil registry office (*Standesamt*) was created for communities, and a registrar was elected to conduct and record each wedding. Church weddings, which until then had been legally binding, now were optional and not legally binding. This system remains the practice in Germany to this day. Despite expressing some doubts about the development, Peter reported in March 1875 that he and a neighbor had served as witnesses for the wedding ceremony of a couple from their neighborhood at the registry office in Horst. It was followed by a wedding service at the church.

- Monetary reform was introduced in 1875. Until then, each formerly independent area of Germany had its own currency. In the former Kingdom of Hanover, which included the Oste Dike region, money was reckoned in thalers, silver coins (*Silbergroschen*), and pennies. Peter's March 1875 letter stated that the national currency would now be imperial marks (*Reichsmarck*), subdivided into 100 pennies per mark. "Old" currency and coins were being called in and exchanged for the new money. In subsequent letters, Peter—understandably but also unfortunately for readers today—often used both systems when citing prices, which adds confusion to understanding relative values.

- Military service in what was called the home guard (*Landsturm*) was now compulsory for men up to the age of 42, while a man could be called to serve in the standing army (*Landwehr*) until age 52.

The Emigrant Letters ♦ 47

Infrastructure improvements and the building of roads was an occasional topic. Peter helped orient his American readers by naming the farm or homeowner where construction was taking place. In a January 1875 letter he described a major project on a large channel near his Breitenwisch farm called the Burgbeck Canal. To this day, the canal is a vital part of water control in the area. It receives runoff water from polders and smaller canals and channels it into the Oste River via a lock along the dike in a place called the Vorwerk.[68] The Vorwerk is still in operation. It is located close to where Johann I and Elisabeth Schlichting's Neuland farm once stood. The upgrade Peter described included dredging and widening of the Burgbeck Canal to accommodate bigger barges for the transporting of peat. Communities and landowners alike were assessed fees to help the government complete the project.

As already mentioned, Peter made efforts to keep the American family updated on the whereabouts of their favorite uncle, Anton Blank. In this group of letters Anton was mentioned twice, first in July 1874, when Peter wrote that Anton had lost a number of beehives the previous winter. Then in the January 1875 letter, Peter stated that at Christmas Anton had visited him and Diedrich in Breitenwisch. It was the first Christmas after the death of Peter's wife. Peter noted that Anton was fattening a pig for slaughter. Aside from that, he wrote, "not much has changed in your old neighborhood [in Neuland]."[69] In the same letter, Peter also noted that he had been charged with maintenance of the Horst locks on the Oste River and received 15 Thaler for the work. He added, "In the cold weather, the locks caused me a lot of work."

---

[68] In Google Maps, enter the coordinates 53.65835, 9.27545.
[69] From other sources, we know that in 1875 Anton was employed as lock keeper at a watermill in the Neuland neighborhood known as Horn, on the Oste River. It was a few miles north of the former Schlichting farm in Neuland. Upon taking up his new job, Anton moved into a house close by the watermill. The watermill was initially built as a means of pumping excess water from polders via a channel to a lock at the dike, from where it would be released into the river at low tide. The watermill was later reconstructed into a gristmill for grinding grain. Anton continued living nearby, though he no longer worked as lock keeper.

In his January 12, 1875, letter, Peter related news about his work and about the Schlichting's uncle, Anton Blank: "Meanwhile, I've had a lot to do. Earlier we had freezing weather, but now it is thawing. I am now charged with maintenance of the Horst locks and receive 15 Thaler for that. In the cold weather, the locks caused me a lot of work. Anton visited us at Christmas. Lately we've had no visits. Anton bought a pig and is fattening it. Not much has changed in your old [Neuland] neighborhood..."

Source: Letter 1875-01-12 Peter S Brtnw to Joh I S MN

Though it is difficult for us to decipher—because of both the language and the distinct *Kurrent* handwriting style he used—Peter's handwriting was very good. Like many other writers in this collection, he took pride in his handwriting. That is significant because neither he nor others among them had received an education that took them beyond an elementary school level.

In his last 1875 letter, written November 8, Peter informed the American family that his and Johann I's sister Anna Margaretha had died on the 2nd of that month at the age of 53. She was buried at the church cemetery in Hechthausen.[70] Anna Margaretha had had a twin sister, Catharina, who had died in 1823 at the age of ten months.

---

[70] Anna Margaretha, who was unmarried, had been living with her sister Metta and family in the village of Kleinwoerden, which is part of the Hechthausen parish.

Peter reported that in the summer of 1875 there had been an abundant harvest of honey. And he wrote that he and Diedrich had undertaken significant repair and renovation work on their house. Finally, he wrote that a new school had been built in Neuland. He ended with, "Now I have one request of you, dear brother and children: that you write to us. You haven't written in a long time."

Farm buildings in 19th century Neuland Oste Dike would have looked much like this one: a half-timbered building structure with thatched roofing. The round stacks in front are firewood curing for the next winter's heating. Peter wrote in his Nov. 8, 1875, letter that during the previous summer he and his brother Diedrich had made significant repairs to their farmhouse: "From the unpainted door on the south side to the northwest corner, we cut a few feet off the supporting posts and replaced them with stone masonry. In all, we used 3,000 stones ... We have enough thatch and reeds [to repair the south roof], and we're thinking of making that repair next summer. We've already had to patch it in places..." The thatching for the roof came from reeds that grow along the banks of the Oste River.

This series includes two letters that are out of the ordinary. While not originally part of our collection, they appeared in *New World Beginnings*.[71] The letters were written by Professor A. Craemer of Concordia College (later Concordia Seminary) in St. Louis, Missouri. They were responses to an inquiry Hinrich must have made about the possibility of entering seminary. This was late in 1874, when Hinrich and his brothers were developing the farm at Jacksonville, Minnesota.

Professor Craemer informed Hinrich that he would have to enter what was called a proseminary in Springfield, Illinois, for one or two years, to prepare for seminary. Seminary itself would be another three years. Craemer's first letter was dated December 13, 1874. He wrote again, on January 20, 1875, recommending that Hinrich speak with "Mr. F. Stuelpnagel so that he may send his recommendations concerning you." At the time, Stuelpnagel was pastor at the West Albany Lutheran church.

Hinrich did not follow through on the professor's recommendation. The existence of the letters, however, reveals a spiritual side to Hinrich that might otherwise be overlooked. In 1874 Hinrich was 37 years old and still unmarried. The farming enterprise was successful, and his brothers and sister were there and could have taken over farming operations. But in the end, he backed away from what would have taken him on a very different course through life. He chose instead to remain a tiller of the soil for the rest of his days.

What adds more interest to these two letters is that in 1902, Hinrich's oldest son, John August, would follow the very course that Prof. Craemer had proposed to Hinrich: proseminary in Springfield, Ill., followed by seminary. John August was ordained and served his entire adult life as a pastor in the Lutheran Church-Missouri Synod. He later wrote extensively and movingly about his father's initially hesitant, but later strongly supportive, response to the son's intention.[72] This will be discussed further in a later chapter.

---

[71] *New World Beginnings for the Schlichting Family*, p. 10.

[72] *As I Remember*, by John August Schlichting, p. 29. Also, *New World Beginnings for the Schlichting Family*, pp. 10-11.

CHAPTER 5

1876-1877

The Move West Begins

Date	Source	Writer in Germany/Recipient	Writer in U.S. / Recipient	Comments
1876 June	Handwritten translation		Sent to Hinrich S, Minn.	Quote for rail and ocean passage to Germany, requested by Hinrich.
1876 June 25	Photocopy		by Hinrich, Claus, Johann II, and Rebecka, Minn.	Affidavit that the four would support their father Johann I, should he return to and remain in Germany.
1876 June 25: Johann I left for Milwaukee bound for Germany but returned to the farm after a few days.				
1876 Oct. 22	original	Peter S and Diedrich S, Breitenwisch, to Johann I & family, Minn.		Everyone was well, incl. Peter's new wife (Maria). Update on Burgbeck Canal work, locks, roads. Anton Blank had worked on the projects. Peter had been asked for information about Anton Schlichting (Johann I's son). Diedrich wrote about his family.
1877 Mar. 25	original	Peter S, Brtnw, to Johann I & family, Minn.		Crops & livestock report. Wet winter left water standing. Anton Blank was unwell in winter. Diedrich's health improved. Peter & wife's winter work. House repairs previous summer.
1877 May 7: Johann II left Minnesota and traveled to Oregon to look for land to buy. Arrived in Portland May 23.				
1877 June 12	original		Claus S, Minn, to Johann II, Ore.	Received Johann's letter. Report on prices, hired workers. Had worked on house foundation. Issue with potato borers. Working new land. Hinrich would write next time.
1877 June 18	photocopy		Johann II, Ore, to Minn. family	Incomplete letter. Reprinted in *New World Beginnings* p. 39. Johann was based in Silverton, Ore. Had been ill, then explored surrounding area.
1877 July 2	original		Claus S, Minn, to Johann II, Ore.	Johann's letter of 6/18 received. Don't exert yourself too much. Had sent the watch. Re. land: homesteading a good idea? 320 acres in Washington Co. seemed a good location.
1877 July 7	original		Hinrich S, Minn, to Johann II, Ore.	Johann's letter of 6/24 received. Glad to read that he was better and was doing carpentry. Responded to J's comments on land prices.
1877 July 20	original		Claus S, Minn, to Johann II, Ore.	Received Johann's 7/4 letter. Had finished "opening" new land, barley harvested, wheat very tall, maple syrup. Approved land possibility in Ore. if not too expensive. Starting a church in Wash. County Ore. would be easier if more Germans came.
1877 July 27	photocopy of English translation		Rebecka S, Minn, to Johann II, Ore.	Barley harvested, wheat was golden, threshing crew coming. Visit from pastor. News from Germany (probably a letter from Peter S)

The Emigrant Letters ♦ 53

Date			From/To	Summary
1877 Sept. 7	original		Claus S, Minn. to Johann II, Ore.	Had been sick—dysentery—now better. Threshing done, some equipment issues. Crop results and prices. Commented on rumors about Pastor Kenter in Oregon.
1877 Sept. 10	original		John Peter Mohrmann, Ore, to Johann II S, Ore.	Response to Johann's letter of 8/13 regarding land to rent and financial arrangements.
1877 Sep. 13	original		Hinrich S, Minn, to Johann II, Ore.	Received Johann's letter. Buy land? Johann would have to see what was best. Working on coming to Oregon.
1877 Sept. 15	original		Hinrich S, Minn, to Johann II, Ore.	Claus would come when he was better. Land parcel near Portland a temp. solution? Buying preferable to renting if price good. Be cautious.
1877 Sept. 21	original		Claus S, Minn, to Johann II, Ore.	Wrote re. financial details for land purchase, sent $1,000, draft good till 12/1. Could send more. Wait till plowing finished before coming west? More thoughts re. the Ore. land in question and housing.
1877 Sept. 29	original		Hinrich S, Minn, to Johann II, Ore.	Rcvd. Johann's letter of 9/16. Asked for more information re. land in Ore. Claus & Rebecka intended to come on 11/7. "Father" (Joh I) mostly positive about Ore. Urged Johann to "buy on your own." Work if possible, do more "looking around" later.
1877 Oct. 2	original		Johann II, Ore, to Minn. family	Wrote many details to aid Claus & Rebecka's travel to Ore., based on his own experience. Suggested meeting them in Silverton.
1877 Oct. 8	original		Hinrich S, Minn, to Johann II, Ore.	Rvcd. Johann's letter of 9/23. Apparent bottleneck of letters. If he needed money to buy land, they could send it; Johann should let them know. Hoped land purchase could be completed. Father seemed inclined to Ore. Father sent $25 to Anton Blank in Germany.
1877 Oct. 9	original		Claus S, Minn, to Johann II, Ore.	Johann's letters arriving regularly. Pleased about land purchase. Planned to leave 11/7, wanted to finish plowing first. Would come via St. Paul.

1877 mid-October, Johann II purchased 265 acres of land in Washington County, Oregon, on the Tualatin River.

1877 November, Claus traveled to Oregon to join Johann II.

Date			From/To	Summary
1877 Nov. 7	original		Claus S, Minn, to Johann II S, Ore.	He was leaving that day for Oregon. Rebecka would come later, spring or summer.
1877 Nov. 16	original		Hinrich S, Minn, to Johann II S, Ore.	Was sending $500 bank draft, payable to "the nearest" Portland bank. Be careful signing it over. By the time it arrived, Claus should have arrived, too.
1877 Nov. 30	original		Hinrich S, Minn, to Johann II S, Ore.	$500 bank draft had been sent on 11/16. Had received a letter from Claus from San Francisco. They were working to sell the property (Parcel A).

1877 Nov. 30	photocopy of English translation		Rebecka S, Minn, to Claus & Joh II, Ore.	Hoped Claus had arrived safely. Misc. news. Weather cold, ink frozen, had to use pencil to write. Geo. Burger would buy their land, $6,500. Hoping to leave for Oregon in spring or summer.
1877 Dec. 9	original	Peter S, Brtnw, to Johann I family, Minn.		Crops and livestock: low honey yield due to storms. Lots of neighborhood news. Anton Blank was well.
1877 Dec. 15	original		Hinrich S, Minn, to Johann II S, Ore.	Received letter that Joh II and Claus were together. Joh. had trouble cashing bank draft; Hinrich offered advice. Also advised to get a P.O. box.
1877 Dec. 16	original	Anton Blank, Neuland, to Johann I, Minn.		Had received their letter, thanked for money. Had decided to find a different house and would welcome more money, if possible. Requested further letters.

In the year 1877, major change was afoot for the Schlichtings. In his journal, Johann II wrote that at least as early as 1873 the family talked about moving to Oregon.[73] They read about a climate that was more temperate, "...in contrast to the western and eastern states." Hinrich had ordered "brochures with descriptions of Oregon and Nebraska." Johann wrote that they were thinking about moving in the spring of 1875.

The plans had to be postponed, however, because of their father's unrelenting desire to return to Germany (see Ch. 3). By mid-1876 this had reached a crisis point. Seeing that their father was determined to follow through on his expressed wish to "go back to his village"—Hinrich had noted this in a September, 1871, letter[74]—his four adult children (Hinrich, Claus, Johann II, and Rebecka) signed an affidavit dated June 26, 1876, which stated that should he in fact travel to and then remain in Germany, they would support him financially. Hinrich even obtained information about passenger fare for the journey by rail from Milwaukee to New York, then by ship to Bremen or Hamburg.[75] The first two documents in the chart above have to do with this.

---

[73] Johann II Schlichting, op. cit., p. 26. The topic is also discussed in *Hinrich*, Chapter 8, pp. 105-114.
[74] 1871-09-abt Hinrich S MN to Claus Joh II S Mlwke.
[75] 1876-06-16 Passage to Germany Quote-Joh I S. The original document is no longer present. What is in our collection is a translation of the original document.

Johann I's four adult children signed this carefully worded affidavit promising to support their father, should he wish to remain in Germany. It reads, "Gilford Township 25 June 1876.

Our father Johann Schlichting a farmer and landowner here in Gilford Township, Wabasha Counti (sic) in the State of Minnesota, is taking a trip to Germany. Should it please him to remain there, we children pledge ourselves to support him in a worthy manner.[76] This is attested by us his four biological children by our signatures. below.

    Hinrich Schlichting
    Claus Schlichting
    Johann Schlichting
    Rebecka Schlichting
Address: Lacke (sic) City
    Wabasha County, Minnesota"

Source: Schlichting Letters Collection, 1876-06-25 Affidavit to Support Johann I S in Germany

In his journal, Johann II wrote that on June 25 of that year, his father "took a trip to Milwaukee." (*machte eine Reise nach Milwauke [sic]*).[77] Given that Hinrich had obtained travel costs for his father that started from Milwaukee, it appears that Johann I intended to follow through on his expressed desire to return to Germany. But in an addendum to the journal Johann II wrote, "Early in summer '76 father actually took off, but he returned after a few days."[78] Adding the words "actually" and "but" indicates that Johann I's children were not expecting their father to return. But these journal entries of Johann II are barebones. This had been an uncomfortable, even distressing, matter and he seems not to have wanted to write much about it. Lurking between the lines, however, was Johann I's children's years-long uncertainty about what their father really wanted or would do if given the opportunity. After he returned to the farm that June, however, the topic of going back to Germany disappeared.

Now that their father was back—and the matter of his returning to Germany settled—Johann II and his brother Claus took the rest of 1876 to plan their Oregon venture. Eventually they settled on the idea that Johann II would travel alone to Oregon in May of 1877. He wrote that while they mentioned the basic plan to their father, they didn't reveal details until the day of his departure grew closer.

---

[76] The word they used was "nourish" (*ernähren*); thus, literally translated, the sentence could read, "...we children pledge ourselves to nourish him in a worthy manner."

[77] Johann II Schlichting, op. cit., p. 24: "On June 25 (1876), father traveled to Milwaukee." Johann II gave no reason for this journey, but it is almost certainly tied to the document the four adult children signed and dated June 26 regarding their father's return to Germany.

[78] Johann II Schlichting, op. cit., p. 32. Johann's German: *Im Frühsommer 76 reiste Vater wirklich loß. kehrte aber in einigen Tagen wieder zurück.*

Merlin Schlichting ♦ 56

In his journal, Johann II added an addendum with background to what he had written earlier about his journey to Oregon. He titled this addendum "The Oregon Story" (Oregon Geschichte) and wrote the following: "Early in the summer of '76 father actually took off, but he returned after a few days. Then Claus and I thought about traveling in fall and winter. Finally, it was decided that I should go alone in spring '77. In mid-November '76 Claus and I spoke a little with father about it, then nothing more until I was actually ready to leave, on May 7, '77. Claus followed in November '77."

Source: Johann II Schlichting Journal Part 3, p. 32

A major complicating factor for any travel westward during 1876/1877 was conflict between Native Americans and white settlers and U.S. troops, including the deadly encounter in June 1876 at Little Bighorn. In 1877, in the very month Johann II was traveling west to Oregon, violence erupted between the Nez Perce and settlers in the Northwest.[79] This was likely a contributing factor to Johann II's choice of route when he traveled west in May—by rail to San Francisco, then by steamship to Portland—and to Claus' route in November.

---

[79] See *Hinrich*, pp. 111-114.

Letters from Germany

The sequence of events just described was interspersed with the arrival of letters from Germany. The first was from Peter Schlichting of Breitenwisch and was dated October 22, 1876. In April of that year, Peter, who had been widowed for more than a year, had married a woman named Maria Junge, herself a widow.[80] In this October letter he wrote that everyone in Breitenwisch was well, adding an update about the massive Burgbeck Canal project nearby, which he had first described in a January 12, 1875, letter. In a development not unfamiliar to us today, Peter stated that costs for the project had risen, and that landowners would have to pay six Thaler more per morgen[81] of land, and even that would not be sufficient. Despite increased costs, however, progress was being made in both the dredging of the canal and the installation of new locks. He also wrote that Anton Blank was working as a day laborer on the locks project, and that he earned one Thaler per day for his work.

In the same letter, Peter mentioned a curious summons he had received from officials seeking information about his brother Johann I's youngest son Anton, who had died in 1871: "I was summoned by the authorities in Himmelpforten to provide information about your deceased son ... I told them that your son Anton had died, and that I knew it from a letter you had sent. But they wanted to know the cause and date of his death. I couldn't tell them because I hadn't read that in the letter you sent. It all had something to do with the military." Seven years after Johann I and his children had emigrated, Prussian officials were looking into the whereabouts of youngest son Anton. Why? In 1876 Anton would have been 22 years old and of prime age for the military draft. It is speculative to write, but perhaps these same officials in Himmelpforten remembered that a relative named Johann Schlichting had escaped service in the Prussian army ten years earlier by fleeing the country.

Peter's brother Diedrich added a few comments of his own, mostly regarding his three adult children, Hinrich, Johann, and Anna. Peter filled out the rest of the page by noting where he had kept his bees that summer: in an area called Villa, just east of Breitenwisch,[82] and sharing other neighborhood news.

Another letter from Peter was dated March 25, 1877. He wrote that Anton Blank had been afflicted with rheumatism and gout during the winter. He was concerned that Anton lived too sparely and that his friends weren't looking after him as well as they should. Peter and Maria were faring well enough, though money was tight. Maria had brought some money into the marriage, and that, plus handwork she created to sell and beehives that Peter crafted—probably with willow branches—kept them going. Finally, he wrote about a home improvement project they had undertaken during the previous summer (1876): new thatching on the south roof of the farmhouse.

---

[80] See, https://ofb.genealogy.net/famreport.php?ofb=burweg&ID=I12812&lang=de

[81] No longer in use, the morgen was at one time a standard measurement of land parcel sizes in Germany. In the Lower Saxony region where Peter lived, one morgen was calculated in the United Nations "World Weights and Measures: Handbook for Statisticians" to be 2,621 square meters, or about 0.65 acre. See, https://www.sizes.com/units/morgen.htm

[82] Located today within the community of Hammah. Google Maps coordinates 53.63780, 9.37269.

Close-up photo of a building that has been roofed with thatch, called Reet (pron. "rate") in German. The thatching material is made of dried bundles of the reeds that grow along the banks of the Oste River. This would have been the material Peter Schlichting used to re-roof his Breitenwisch farm home in 1876.

Thatched roofs are very durable, and they provide good insulation. However, they are expensive to install and are subject to high insurance rates. For those reasons, they are not seen as often today as they once were.

The Move to Oregon

Almost all letters in our collection from the year 1877 were written or received by members of the American family. As noted above, Johann II left Minnesota for Oregon on May 7, 1877, and arrived in Portland on May 23. While we don't know his exact route, we can reconstruct it to a considerable degree from a letter he sent back to the Minnesota family on October 2 of that year.[83] From this and other letters he wrote that fall, it is clear that he was anticipating the arrival of the rest of the family in Oregon by year's end. In that long October 2 letter, Johann sent detailed advice for their journey west, including hotel names and even names of coach drivers they should seek out.

---

[83] "1877-10-02 Johann II S OR to MN Family"

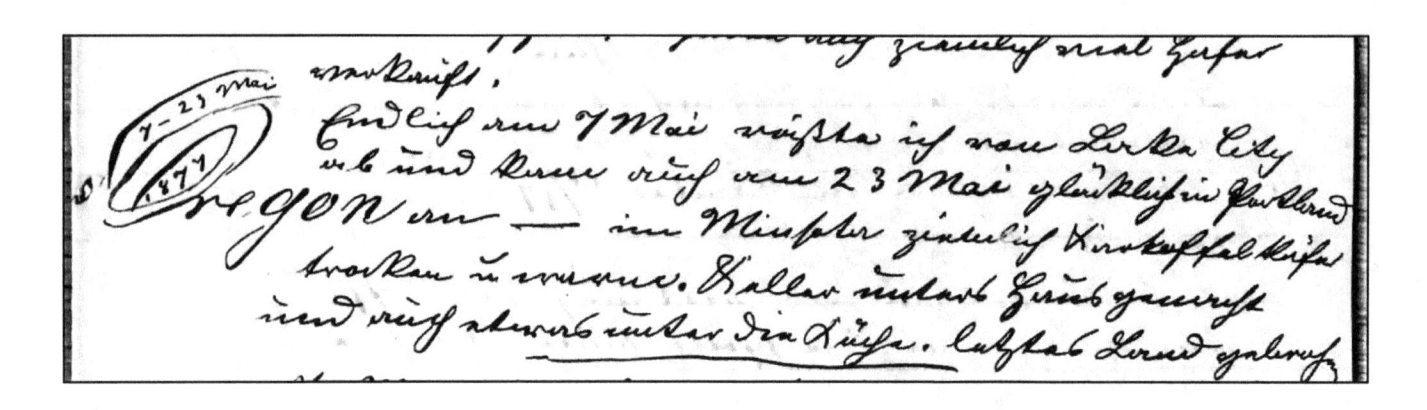

Johann II added a flourish to his journal entry about his departure from Lake City and arrival in Portland. He wrote, "Finally, on May 7 I departed from Lake City, arriving happily on May 23 in Portland Oregon"
   Source: Johann II Schlichting Journal Part 3, p. 25

Letters exchanged among the American Family in 1877

Letters exchanged among family members during 1877 are preoccupied with the search for land to buy in Oregon. Almost immediately after Johann II arrived in Portland on May 23, he began that search. From Portland he traveled south to Silverton, which became his base of operations.[84]

On June 12, Claus wrote Johann II to update him on the situation on the Minnesota farm. Crop and livestock sales in spring had been good. They were making repairs to the basement of the farmhouse. Potato borers were affecting their crop; picking them off the foliage by hand was the best control they had. Cool weather had slowed current crop growth, and they had nearly finished breaking more new land.

Johann II's incomplete June 18 letter, written from Silverton, is reproduced in *New World Beginnings* on p. 39 along with a hand-drawn map. He reported having been ill with what was called "gall fever," perhaps from a waterborne pathogen. Once he recovered, he traveled from Silverton, along with "3 Germans," who claimed homesteads along the way. Unlike his traveling companions, Johann II felt that the area would not be suitable for farming, and that he would write a description of his subsequent travels. Unfortunately, that part of his letter is missing. But his hand-drawn map helps us understand his movements through the area, and it identifies towns, roads, and settlements. It is reproduced here.

---

[84] In Google Maps, type in coordinates, 45.00647, -122.77634.

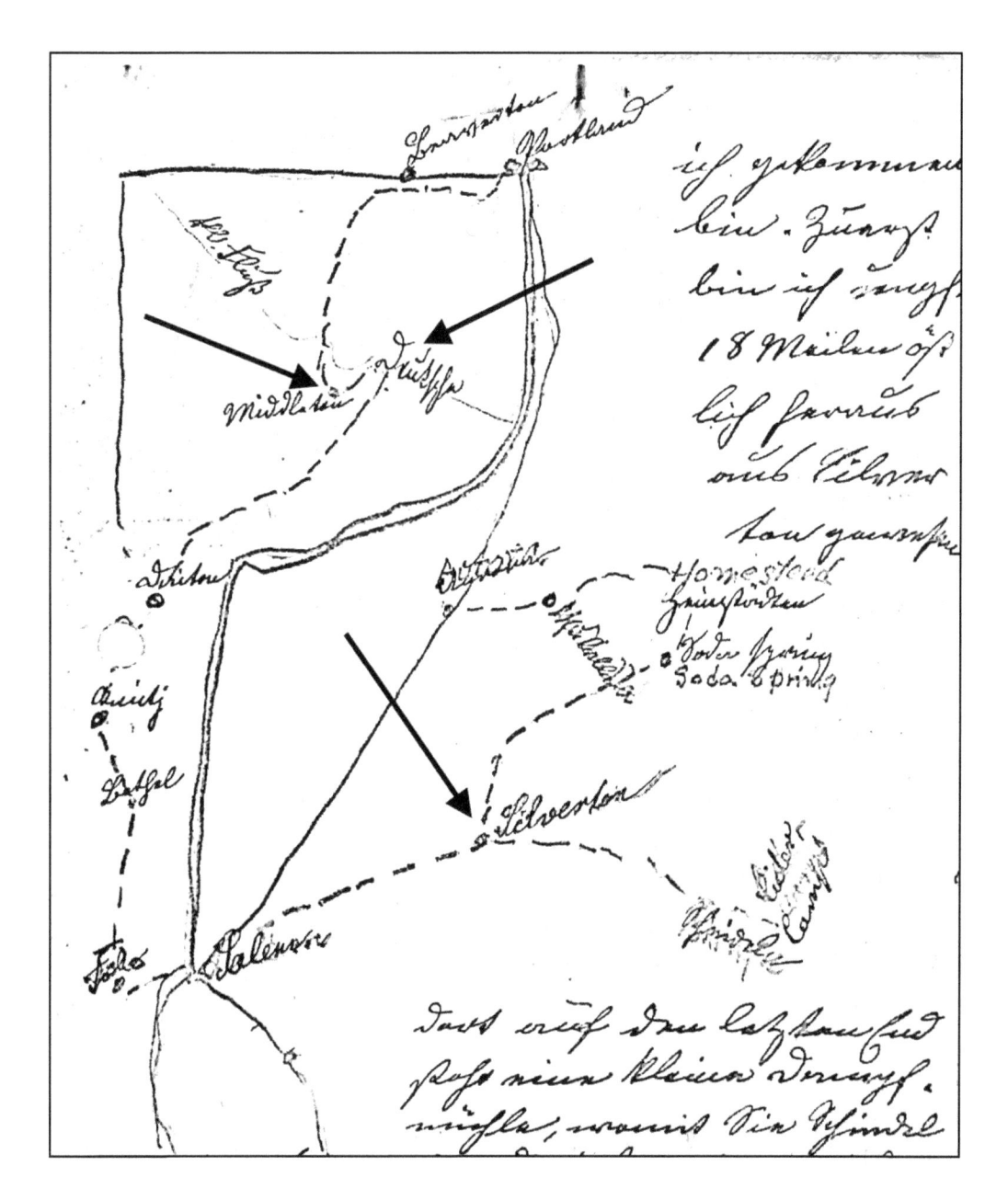

In his June 18, 1877, letter, Johann II drew a map to show his first travels in Oregon. He indicated his route with a broken line. (At some time, another person wrote over some of Johann's words, making them a challenge to decipher.) Beginning in Portland (top, next to Beaverton), he traveled south to Middleton (top arrow left). There he found a settlement of Germans (Deutsche, top arrow right). He continued south through Dayton, Amity, Bethel, and Eola, then east to Salem, and on to Silverton (lower arrow). From Silverton he first ventured southeast (about 18 miles, as he wrote in the letter) and found a small steam mill that produced shingles (bottom right, Schindeln). He also identified a place called Cider Camp nearby. Although the rest of the letter is now missing, this drawing indicates that he returned to Silverton, then ventured north to Soda Spring, and an area where there were homesteads. Johann's German word appears to be Heimstödten (or Heimstädten), a transliteration of the English "homesteads." From there he traveled west to Molalla (name obscured), and finally to Aurora (also obscured). He soon took up temporary residence in Silverton and from there wrote numerous letters to his family in Minnesota.

The Emigrant Letters ♦ 61

The exchange of letters that year between Oregon and Minnesota was intense. On July 2, Claus wrote from the Minnesota farm to Johann II in Oregon, confirming receipt of Johann's June 18 letter as well as others. He wrote that it was taking about ten days for Johann's letters to arrive. He advised his brother, "Don't exert yourself too much with work ... There's no need to run all over at this time. You have enough money; otherwise, you must write us." He added that he had "sent the watch," and ended by writing, "Homesteading might not be such a bad thing," and, "The 320 acres owned by the German in Washington County is probably a good location. Claus ended the letter by writing, "With God's help, all will go well." This or similar expressions of faith and trust in God appeared frequently in letters.

In a short July 7 letter, Hinrich sent an encouraging response to what Johann apparently had written him: that Johann had found carpentry work to support himself while he continued his search for land to buy.

During all this time, Johann had been based in Silverton, which is in Marion County. But his interest was drawn back north, to Washington County and the community called Middleton, where according to his map he had found a settlement of Germans. His letters, as well as comments from Claus and Hinrich in their letters, show that he was spending more time in that area. The subject of available farmland in Middleton was brought up again by Claus in a July 20 letter. He wrote, "It would be excellent if land were still available from the Low German man (*den platt Deutschen*) in Washington County. But if it costs more than $10 per acre at the upper limit, it would no longer be affordable. We didn't understand how much the Low German man's land cost."

In the same letter, Claus responded to news Johann II must have sent about efforts being made in Middleton to start a German Lutheran congregation. Claus felt it would be easier "...if more Germans come." The founding of a German Lutheran congregation would indeed be realized in 1878, and Johann II came to be closely involved. In his journal, he included a lengthy summary of the congregation's early development.[85] The congregation eventually became St. Paul Lutheran Church. Both Johann II and Claus would have important roles in its formation, as well as in the construction of the first sanctuary.

Two 1877 letters written by their sister Rebecka have also survived, though only as typed English translations. Writing on July 27 from Minnesota to Johann II, she described preparing for a threshing crew and reported a visit from their pastor. A letter had arrived from Uncle Peter in Germany—not in our collection—and Rebecka conveyed some of its news to Johann, including word about their uncle, Anton Blank. Then she wrote snippets about day-to-day farm matters: the "old long-legged cow" had eaten some of their garden cabbage; the horse was sick; and they had baby chicks.

Claus wrote again on September 7. He had been sick with dysentery most of the summer, but "some bitter medicine" he took for eight days helped him recover enough to help with the harvest.[86] He added an encouraging comment about land Johann seemed to be considering for purchase: "The land you can buy there seems right (*notwendig*).[87] It seems good to me, even if not all of it is desirable (underlined by Claus). We

---

[85] Johann II Schlichting, op. cit., pp. 28a-28b.
[86] Claus, and probably other family members, put considerable stock in homeopathic medicine. Johann II wrote about it in his journal (Op. cit., p.26).

[87] Claus wrote "necessary" (*notwendig*). But from the next sentence, his meaning seems to have been that despite any drawbacks it might have, the land Johann had found was what they were seeking; hence, the "right" land.

need to talk soon about going out there." Might this have been the land the Johann eventually bought? It can't be stated with certainty, but it seems possible.

In the same letter, Claus commented about the pastor who had been contacted to help form the Lutheran congregation in Middleton, August Kenter. Kenter had arrived there from Minnesota, though without the recommendation of the Minnesota Synod of the Lutheran Church-Missouri Synod. Claus indicated that rumors were circulating that Kenter supposedly had misappropriated some money in Minnesota (*etwas Geld unterschlagen haben soll*). But Claus thought the rumors questionable (or as he put it, were "thin") and expressed confidence that the congregation in Middleton would soon come together. He added that they (the Minnesota family) should send some money soon to support the effort. "If it's near Portland," he noted, "it is well located, near the primary market. Now all is in God's name, and it will succeed (underlined by Claus)." Pastor Kenter served the Middleton congregation from its founding in 1878 until 1883.[88]

Johann II received an interesting letter, dated September 10, from a man named Johann Peter Mohrmann, who farmed in Middleton in Washington County. Mohrmann referred to questions Johann II had asked him in an August 13 letter—not in our collection—by suggesting a few possibilities of land to rent. Incidentally, the surname Mohrmann appears several times in Johann II's journal report about the formation of the Lutheran congregation in Middleton. In the 2003 booklet printed on the occasion of the 125th anniversary of the congregation's founding, John Peter Mohrmann was named as one of the founding members.[89] The letter-writer of Sept. 10, 1877, was almost certainly the same man. It should be noted that the envelope for this September 10 letter was sent to Johann II in Silverton, meaning that his move to Washington County, and Middleton, had not yet happened. Letters in our collection written as late as October 9 were all sent to Johann in Silverton. The first letter sent to him in Middleton was dated November 7.

On September 13 Hinrich sent a short note to Johann II: "As for buying land, you will have to see what is best. We are working and preparing to come, but it is a slow process."

Two days later, on September 15, Hinrich wrote again to say that Claus would be on his way west once he was well enough to travel. The "land parcel near Portland" seemed a good temporary or interim (*vorläufig*) solution, but Hinrich urged Johann to continue to look around, and he should not be too quick to rent anything—he clearly favored buying rather than renting. And of course, Johann should do nothing "in the heat of the moment." The land near Portland Hinrich mentioned in this letter was almost certainly the same land Johann eventually bought. That is underscored by what Claus wrote to Johann just a week later.

Claus wrote that letter on September 21. As Hinrich had done in his September 15 letter, Claus encouraged Johann regarding the land parcel he had described: "As for buying the land, we think you should. You can apply a little pressure by saying that you have another parcel in mind, or some other business. We're not sure either what is best. If his small house is still there, we could surely live in it for a while."

The "small house" Claus mentioned points to that property as the land Johann bought in October. The previous owner had built a cabin not far from the Tualatin River. In 2016, during a family gathering at the Oregon farm, then owners Robert and Elanna Schlichting took us guests on a

---

[88] St. Paul Lutheran Church, Sherwood, Oregon, 125th Anniversary booklet, pp. 4-9.

[89] Op. cit., p. 3.

tour around the farm. We took in views of the tree-lined river at the base of the gentle slope of the field. They also took us to the place where Robert told us the cabin had once stood. It now is a farm field. As we absorbed that information and enjoyed the views on a pleasant summer day, off in the distance to the east we also could see the snow-covered slopes of Mount Hood. It was an inviting and pleasant view. What we could not see, of course, was the land as it looked to Johann II in that fall of 1877: raw land partially cleared of its virgin forest but still littered with stumps and the remnants of trees—not what most people would consider inviting. Johann, however, must have seen promise.

Johann's later journal entry about the purchase was brief and to the point. He wrote, "In mid-October I bought land in Oregon, about 265¼ acres...in Washington County on the Tualatin River, 14 miles from Portland..."[90] The purchase was completed in January 1878.[91] Brothers Johann II and Claus became occupants of the cabin. After the rest of the family (their father Johann I, Rebecka, and domestic worker Minna Parsohn) arrived in June of 1878, the whole family lived together in the cabin until 1881, when a new house was built higher and farther away from the river (where the farm buildings now stand). John August Schlichting recalled the cabin in his memoir: "In the beginning of 1878 Uncle Johann, Uncle Claus, Grandfather (Johann I), and Aunt Rebecka lived in a small house down by the Tualatin River."[92]

Sometimes these old letters present readers today with a genuine bonus. This letter is one of those. At the top of the second page of Claus' Sept. 21 letter, Johann II used the space to write out his plan for the week of October 8-12, 1877, Monday through Friday. It gives us a look into his busy schedule, which included looking at more land, further contact with Mohrmann, a trip to Oregon City, and a visit to the State Fair in Salem.

---

[90] Johann II Schlichting, op. cit., p. 25.
[91] Johann II Schlichting, op. cit., p. 27. Johann wrote, "On January 15 the deed for the land on the Tualatin River was signed with Moore in Oregon City..."
[92] John August Schlichting, op. cit., p. 14.

In the top margin of the Sept. 21, 1877, letter he received from Claus, Johann II wrote out his schedule for the week of Oct. 8-12:

8   Mon. morning
     11 a.m., Gervais
     3 p.m., in Oregon City

9   Tues. noon
     Mohrmann
     afternoon, look at land

10 Wednesday
     look at other land
     160 acres
     shells (uncertain word)

11 Thurs noon
     Oregon City

12 Friday a.m.
     Salem Fair

     Sat

Schlichting Letters Collection, 1877-09-21 Claus MN to Joh II S Silverton OR.

Meanwhile, the letter exchange continued. Hinrich wrote on September 29, referring to a September 16 letter from Johann—not in the collection—and asking for more information about land. He wrote that Claus and "Becka" intended to travel west on November 7, then added, "Father is mostly positive about Oregon." As for the land in question, Hinrich wrote, "As long as you have work, we prefer [buying] to renting. My idea is that you go ahead and buy it yourself. I've written about that, also the way to obtain each parcel of land. Later when you're not working somewhere, you can do more looking around." Even though a land purchase now seemed likely, Hinrich urged Johann to keep looking for more land.

Hinrich ended by writing that he was looking into possibilities for selling, referring to the first farm they had bought in Minnesota (Parcel A). We learn from a late November letter from Rebecka, that first farm, Parcel A, was in the process of being sold to George and Theresa Burger for $6,500. The sale would be finalized in January. The mailing envelope for this September 29 letter is still present. It was postmarked September 30 and addressed to Johann II in Silverton, Marion Co., Oregon.

On the envelope back, Johann had sketched a few floor plans and written what appears to be a shopping list.

The Emigrant Letters ♦ 65

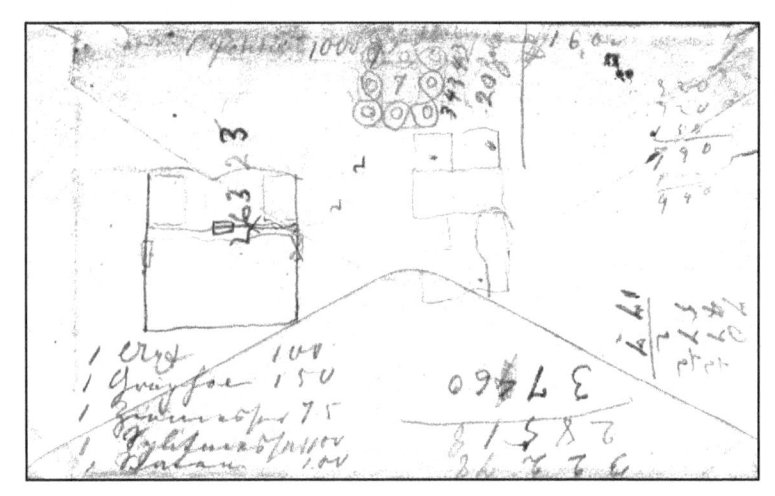

Johann used the back of the envelope to draw a few floorplans and to make a shopping list, lower left (dollar signs added):
1 Ax, $1.00
1 Grubhoe, $1.50
1 Draw knife, $.75
1 Splitting knife, $1.00
1 Spade, $1.00
Schlichting Letters Collection: 1877-09-29
Hinrich MN to Joh II Silverton OR

Johann II was anticipating—no doubt eagerly—that Claus and Rebecka would arrive in Oregon yet that fall. On October 2 he wrote them the long letter already mentioned (at six pages the longest in our collection). Given the uncertainties of travel in the fall of 1877, Johann wrote his recommendations for travel that involved rail, coach, and steamship. Such a plan would largely replicate his own journey the previous May. From this letter, it is also clear that he would soon be moving from Silverton, so he wrote with a few contingencies in mind: "In Portland I've always stayed at the New York Hotel (also German). It isn't far from where you disembark [from the steamship].—Because things are uncertain, and because a letter exchange is so slow, I suggest the following: In Salem there is the Benton House, a very good German hotel. If I should leave Silverton sooner than I plan to, or if some of you should come sooner, I will leave instructions behind, or I will send them, etc. I also could leave instructions at the New York Hotel in Portland." He continued with word about the potential land purchase: "I wrote to the man regarding the land around Portland, but I haven't received a reply. I have work [here] for about another week. On October 8 the state fair begins in Salem. I'd like to go see it if I have the opportunity..." The last comment reminds us that the week's calendar Johann jotted on the back of Claus' September 29 letter included a visit to the state fair in Salem.[93]

How closely Claus—the only Minnesotan to travel west that fall—followed Johann's suggestions cannot be stated with certainty, but we know that he traveled via San Francisco (see Hinrich's letter of November 30 below).

Hinrich wrote on October 8 with the assurance that if Johann committed to buying land, Hinrich could send money, though the preference would be to wait with sending anything until Johann was settled at a permanent address. He asked Johann to send word about financial arrangements. Reassuringly, he also noted that despite some uncertainty, "[Father] is doing well and also seems well inclined toward Oregon." In a postscript he added, in pencil, "Father sent $25.00 to [Uncle] Anton Blank [in Germany]. Anton might be moving ... since the area is good enough." That he did send the money is evidenced in a December letter from Anton, which is described below.

The very next day, October 9, Claus wrote. It is apparent they had received word that Johann had made an agreement to purchase the land

---

[93] In 1877, fairgoers had a chance to see exhibits of recent inventions: Thomas Edison's phonograph and Alexander Graham Bell's telephone. See, https://www.statesmanjournal.com/story/news/local/oregon/2015/08/22/years-oregon-state-fair-memory-lane/32223239/

(though such a letter is not in the collection): "We were quite pleased that you had bought the land or will shortly if possible. If that is so, it is a good purchase. We will soon be on our way, and we will be able to talk in person ... On November 7 we must be on our way. Like you, we'll come by way of St. Paul. That seems the best."

On November 7, Claus wrote that the day of his departure had arrived: "As God wills, today, the 7th of November, I depart from here in God's name, healthy and with good courage...Rebecka is not going yet; hopefully, she and the others can leave together next spring or summer. This letter will probably arrive before I do."

Hinrich wrote on November 16, that he was sending a $500 bank draft from the Lake City bank, "payable to the nearest bank in Portland..." He cautioned his brother to be careful with signing over the draft to the seller: "[The bank] might charge $1 for their services...Be very cautious with signing the draft. Better to pay the dollar and be sure everything is in order. By then Claus will be there as well."

Hinrich wrote again, on November 30, telling Johann II that the $500 had been sent by bank draft on Nov. 16. He also stated that they had received a letter from Claus, from San Francisco— an indication that Claus was following the same route to Oregon that Johann II had taken in May.

The second of Rebecka's letters that year was written to Johann II the same day, November 30. She hoped Claus had arrived. Weather had turned cold; in fact, the ink had frozen, so she had to write the letter with a pencil. The most important news was that a man named George Burger[94] had agreed to buy their first farm (named Parcel A in *Hinrich*), for $6,500 and that if all went well, the family could make the trip west the following spring or summer. She also commented that "The people here all want to go to the Western Shore." She ended her letter with a reminder that in the meantime, farm life continued as usual: that day, with the help of John Krone, perhaps a neighbor, they had butchered a 416-pound hog.

Having left Minnesota on November 7, Claus arrived in Oregon sometime later that month to join his brother on their newly acquired property in Middleton. A December 15 letter from Hinrich expressed gratitude that Claus and Johann II were together again. He also expressed concern about Johann II's difficulty with the bank drafts Hinrich sent—they sometimes were being returned. Apparently, Johann had written as much, though what he meant by "being returned" (or "sent back") is not clear. Johann might have written Hinrich about it in the same letter that informed Hinrich of Claus' arrival—a letter not in the collection. The thought development in Hinrich's letter is also difficult to follow.

It is remarkable that this long series of letters between Minnesota and Oregon has been preserved. Once the purchase agreement was signed in October, the wheels for the rest of the Minnesota family to move west were set in motion, though the move did not proceed quite as they had anticipated.

Land in Oregon had now been purchased. It is likely that the two brothers spent that winter in the little cabin above the Tualatin River. In spring 1878 they traveled together to explore other possible land acquisitions, in northern and eastern Oregon and southeastern Washington territory, at one point even extending into Idaho territory.[95] But apart from finding a few horses to buy, they found no land as attractive to them as the property Johann II had purchased in Middleton.

---

[94] The warranty deed appears in *Hinrich* on p. 223, but Theresa Burger was the only buyer named.

[95] Johann II Schlichting, op. cit., p. 27.

Two More 1877 Letters from Germany

Two December letters from Germany round out the 1877 group. The first was from Peter and was written on December 9.[96] In this letter he wrote about prices for crops and livestock. He and brother Diedrich had sold a sizeable harvest of apples and pears, and for 20 Thaler they also sold pigs they had fattened. There was news from the neighborhood, including word about the current inhabitants of the Schlichtings' old farmhouse in Neuland: "Carsten Nagel is still living in your house and his mother runs the household. Anton [Blank] is there, too. He has bees, but he doesn't do any more fishing."

Of note were changes at the wind-powered watermill in Neuland-Horn along the Oste River. The mill had a new owner named Schroeder, who in turn had leased it to a teacher named Bartels. The windmill had been rebuilt and repurposed. Now instead of pumping excess water from the polders into the Oste River, it would serve as a wind-powered gristmill for grain. Within a few years, Anton Blank would build a house of his own on the inner dike near the mill. This will be discussed in a later chapter.

A second letter was written on December 16 by Anton Blank to his brother-in-law Johann I, who was still in Minnesota.[97] He began his letter, "Dear Brother-in-Law, from your letter I see that you would like to know how things are here. I can tell you that everything is almost the same as ever. As for myself, I am well, although I was sick from three weeks before Christmas until Easter and couldn't eat anything" (Peter had written about that in his March 25 letter). He then wrote that he had received the money Johann I had sent (the $25 noted in Hinrich's October 8th letter) and what it had amounted to in the new Prussian currency: 102 Marks and 50 pennies. The money had arrived "at just the right time," seeing as Anton was thinking of acquiring a different house. He added that he would welcome further gifts for that purpose. This topic would be raised again.

---

[96] 1877-12-09 Peter S Brtnw to Joh I S MN

[97] 1877-12-16 Anton Blanck Nlnd to Joh I S MN

Chapter 6

1878-1879

Oregon!

Date	Source	Writer in Germany/Recipient	Writer in U.S. / Recipient	Comments
1878 January 7, Hinrich sold Parcel A farm in Wabasha County, Minn. for $6,500. Family was living on Parcel B.					
1878 January 15, Johann II's purchase of land in Middleton (Sherwood), Ore. was recorded, $1,591.50.				
1878 Feb 8	photocopy		Rebecka S., Minn, to Claus, Joh II, Ore.	Sent 200 lb. box, cost $11.30, would bring bed. Church construction. F. Langer had bought their house. Had butchered pigs. People coming to buy things. Mild winter.
1878 Feb 9	original		Hinrich S, Minn, to Claus, Joh II, Ore.	Would send $500, more next week. Would settle debt in Mlwke. Comments re. clearing land, hiring help. Advice on buying horses. Advice to erect buildings to protect equipment. Don't buy lightning rods. Oregon land they bought is "gold."
1878 Feb 21	original		Joh II S, Ore, to Hinrich S, Minn.	C&J both well. Rain hindering clearing land. "Prairie" land preferable. Commented about area beyond Walla Walla along Columbia R.
1878 Mar 25	original		Joh II S, Washington Territory, to Claus S, Ore.	Described land near Walla Walla, discussed ways to claim or own land, had signed letters of intent. Discussed travel costs from Omaha. Wanted to explore area around W.W.
1878, early spring	original		Hinrich S, Minn, to Claus, Joh II, Ore.	Good weather, might seed soon. Received letter re. wet weather in Ore. Sent bank drafts, two for each brother at $500/draft.
1878 Apr 7	original		Hinrich S, Minn, to Claus, Joh II, Ore.	Noted their receiving money he had sent. Understood Joh II was in Walla Walla. Travel date to Oregon not yet certain.
1878 Apr 16	original	Peter S, Breitenwisch, to Johann I family, Minn.		March storm caused house damage and flooding. Anton Blank was buying wood to build a house. Crops and livestock report. Sister Metta's family all well.
1878 Apr 20	photocopy		Joh II S, Ore, to Hinrich S, Minn.	He had returned from Walla Walla; on the way he had looked at land in Umatilla County. Offered advice on the route for the family to take west, included map.
1878 May 4	original		Hinrich S, Minn, to Claus, Joh II, Ore.	He had received letter from W.W. & news that Joh II had returned to the Middleton farm. Travel dates west not yet certain.
1878 June, Johann I, Hinrich, Rebecka, and domestic helper Minna Parsohn moved from Minnesota to Oregon and remained there, except for Hinrich, who in July returned to the Minnesota farm.				

The Emigrant Letters ♦ 69

1878 July 5	original		Johann II S, NE Ore, to Claus S, Middleton, Ore.	He and Hinrich were traveling in NE Oregon and had arrived in Milton[-Freewater]. Was unsure where the Indians were; he was staying far away from them because of hostilities.
1878 July 22	original		Hinrich S, Middleton, Ore, to Joh II S, NE Ore.	He had returned (to Middleton) from his own travels. Advised Johann to abandon land search and return to Middleton. Warned of "alkali sickness."
1878 late summer	original		Hinrich S, Minn, to Claus S, Ore.	Hinrich back in Minn., learned that Johann II had returned to Middleton. Crop prices. Father (Johann I) wanted to send money to Germany, using earned interest; asked whether Johann II or Claus preferred to send it.
Undated, late 1878 into 1879	original		Hinrich S, Minn, to Claus Joh II S, Ore.	Hinrich was against renting more land, favored improving the Oregon land already bought. Suggested cattle raising. Noted cold Minn. winters; speculated about his future and joining them in Oregon. Good, clean land is the best.
1879 Jan	original		Hinrich S, Minn, to Claus Joh II S, Ore.	He would send "things" soon. Mild winter weather. They should write if they needed money or other things. Paid balance on the quarter section (Parcel B). Stick with one bank. Don't hurry to buy land; use caution.
1879 Mar 25	original		Hinrich S, Minn, to Claus, Joh II, Ore.	Discussed money already sent, would send more around June. They should give him plenty of notice when money was needed.
1879 Sept	original		Hinrich S, Minn, to Claus, Joh II, Ore.	Good that Claus better again. They had to decide about renting. Make improvements on your place. Don't hurry. Prices low.

The year 1878 began with two important transactions. On January 7 in Minnesota, Hinrich completed the sale of the first property he had bought, near Jacksonville, Minn. (named Parcel A in *Hinrich*).[98] He sold it to Teresa and George Burger for $6,500. Hinrich, his father Johann I, Rebecka and a young girl named Minna Parsohn[99] were living on the second property he had bought in 1874 (named Parcel B), a few miles away.

The other transaction, on January 15, was the completion of Johann II's purchase of about 260 acres of land on the Tualatin River, south of Portland in the community of Middleton (now Sherwood). He wrote in his journal that the total price was $1,591.50. He made a small down payment and mortgaged the balance.[100] The purchase was the culmination of numerous letter exchanges between him, Claus, and Hinrich during 1877 (see Ch. 5). Both Hinrich and Claus had encouraged Johann II to buy land to farm, rather than renting it. Letters we still have, along with his own journal, show that Johann had investigated several possibilities for purchasing land before settling on the Middleton location.

Claus had arrived in Oregon in November 1877. From then on, he and Johann II began working to develop their new property. But for a while they also continued looking at additional land sites to the north and east of Middleton, in Oregon and in Washington territory just across the Columbia River. In his journal, for example, Johann II noted that between March 21 and April

---

[98] A copy of the warranty deed is reprinted in *Hinrich*, p. 223.

[99] While we do not know Minna's precise age, in his journal Johann II noted that she was confirmed in June 1880 at the Oregon church (p. 30). This would indicate that she probably was 14 or 15 years old at the time.

[100] Johann II Schlichting, op.cit., p. 25. Also in *New World Beginnings*, p. 40.

14, 1878, he traveled to Walla Walla in Washington territory. This will be discussed below.

Johann II's first journal entry for 1878 reads: "Minnesota and Oregon – 1878. On 15 January we signed ("made") the deed with Moore in Oregon City for the land on the Tualatin [R]iver. (see year '77) On 12 March I paid the $300 note to Moore with 2 months interest, [amounting to] $306." (Johann II Schlichting Journal Part 3, p. 27)

On February 8, sister Rebecka wrote from Minnesota to her brothers in Oregon to update them on preparations for the rest of the family's anticipated move west. She wrote that they had shipped a 200-pound container to them in late January ("postage" was $11.30). Among other things, it contained brushes for Claus, an umbrella, and "things we forgot to send." But they hadn't sent the bed, seeing as they still needed it. She also wrote that a man named Ferdinand Langer had bought their house.[101]

Rebecka also commented that construction of a Lutheran church in Jacksonville was progressing, with lumber and brick now on hand and work ready to commence as soon as weather allowed. Her brother Hinrich was very much involved in the construction of the church building.[102] Meanwhile in Oregon, both Claus and Johann II were involved in the formation of a Lutheran congregation in Middleton. Johann II devoted two full pages in his journal to describing it.[103] Beyond that, nothing is noted in any other letters about the church building activities of the three brothers.

The next day, February 9, Hinrich wrote at length to Claus and Johann II. He began by writing that he would be sending them a total of $2,000, and he suggested that they invest it to earn interest. He also brought up a situation involving an unnamed man in Milwaukee, to whom a balance of $300 was owed for a land transaction (he offered no details; Claus and Johann II doubtless knew about it). Hinrich wrote that he would send that money in spring, and that there was no reason for either Claus or Johann II to concern themselves with it. Other topics in the letter included:

- He urged the brothers not to work too hard at clearing land themselves, but rather to hire workers, either by contract or as day laborers.
- He offered advice on buying horses: buy them at young ages and try them out for a day

---

[101] As it turned out, this was incorrect. Rebecka was referring to a sale of the Parcel B Minnesota property, where the family was then living. Hinrich, who was the owner, had considered selling it but then decided against it. Both Rebecka and Johann II were under the impression that Hinrich had sold it. For a more complete discussion, see *Hinrich*, Ch. 9.
[102] See, *Hinrich*, pp. 116-120.
[103] Johann II Schlichting, op. cit., pp. 28a-28b.

first, watching their gait and lines, and beware of the quality of horse gear and wagons.
- He advised them to get their "things" under protection in barn or house, but "Don't try to build too fancy" (*nicht zu schön*). He then added a curious comment: "Don't have anything to do with insurance companies." As an example, he referred to the encouragement by insurers to install lightning rods, of which he disapproved.[104] He called the salesmen "Fancy Beggars"—*Feine Bettler* in German—using oversized letters for emphasis.
- He wrote that when he sent money, it would be $2,000, and that there would be no more until fall.
- He offered brotherly advice about money: "How you manage the money is your business. But be careful and thrifty. You don't need to work hard, but of course, it's also true that one person can work very hard to achieve something, and the other one can destroy it through carelessness or stupidity."

Hinrich ended this letter with a solid endorsement of the purchase of the land on the Tualatin River, and he encouraged them to continue looking for more: "You have found gold in that pile of land (265½ acres). Maybe you can add to it, or buy more, or stake a claim..." It should be noted that at this point in time, Hinrich had not yet seen the Oregon property and thus had no idea of the challenges facing the family—and his brothers specifically—in clearing the land and converting it into cropland. It wasn't until he brought his father and sister to Oregon in the summer of 1878 that he saw those challenges firsthand.

Later that same month, on February 21, Johann II wrote to Hinrich, informing him that constant rain was slowing the clearing of trees and stumps on the land they had bought. Still, he noted, "As far as clearing is concerned, our land is among the best in the area." He also added that, given the choice, they would rather buy land in the "Prairie" area. In an email from August 2020, Oregon descendant Robert Schlichting explained that Johann might have been referring to the French Prairie area in the Willamette River valley. Robert noted that by the time Johann II and Claus arrived in Oregon, most of this prime land was already sold or was prohibitively expensive.

From Johann II's journal, we learn that he traveled north and east from Middleton for about a month in March and April of that year.[105] This February 21 letter indicates that he also had done some prior research about the area around Walla Walla in Washington Territory and extending as far as southwest Idaho Territory, seeking land for possible investment on or near the Columbia River. His final comment was, "The Snake River is navigable to Lewiston (Idaho)."

---

[104] Hinrich's dislike of lightning rods is hard to understand, given their effectiveness at preventing lightning-caused barn or house fires. A possible explanation is that his ire was aimed not at actual insurance companies, but rather at traveling salesmen who sold things like lightning rods as "insurance" and charged exorbitant rates. In his letter, Hinrich went on to write, "[Avoiding them] will spare your family interest [payments] and lots of money (using '$x' as a symbol), along with a lot of effort and talk."

[105] Johann II Schlichting op. cit., p. 27 (also in *New World Beginnings*, p. 40).

In his Feb. 21, 1878, letter to his brother Hinrich, Johann II described his plan to explore areas east of the Middleton area and included a map he sketched. For orientation, note "The Dalles" in the left corner and the Columbia River marking the divide between Oregon and Washington. Idaho (misspelled Idoha) is in the upper right corner, with the Blue Mountains (blauen Berge) written in to the south.

On this first page of the letter, Johann wrote what is noted above: "Both of us are still very healthy, praise God, and we hope you are as well ... It has been raining here for quite some time, and for that reason we haven't been able to do much grubbing (clearing). So, I can't say how easy or difficult it is, or how much it might cost. As far as clearing is concerned, our land is among the best in the area. Certainly, if we could get land in Prairie and if everything went well, we would rather do that." Schlichting Letters Collection: 1878-02-21 Joh II OR to Hinrich S MN.

Johann II's trip to that area east of Middleton began about a month later. On March 25, he wrote to brother Claus in Middleton that he had arrived in Walla Walla and had walked an hour's distance beyond the edge of town. He observed wheat "already a foot tall, and as black and strong as I have ever seen. The soil is fairly light and dusty. I hear that along the Snake River the soil is black and more fertile." He wrote extensively about the various ways a person could claim land, and he added that for $3.75 he had signed letters of intent for four townships along the Snake River.[106]

Thinking of the rest of the family coming west, he added that the Northwestern Stage line was charging an $85 fare from Omaha, with just one travel class, and a travel time of six days. But he wanted to get further information before writing anything more about it to Hinrich. He also wrote that the next day he intended to walk by way of "Daiton" to "Jack" (Dayton to Jackson), and that it was a long way. Google Maps shows Dayton to be about 30 miles, and Jackson almost 50 miles, from Walla Walla, a long way indeed. Johann ended the letter by observing that grass hadn't grown very tall yet, but that the peach trees were in bloom. The letter, incidentally, was written in pencil.

A short, undated note follows Johann's March 25th letter. It was written by Hinrich to his brothers in Oregon. Based on Hinrich's noting that weather in Minnesota had been mild and that he might soon be sowing seed, it likely was written in early spring, probably late March. He wrote, "Received your last letter that it is wet (Johann had written that on Feb. 21), and that you want to buy young horses." While there is no letter in the collection expressing a desire to buy horses, Hinrich's comment corresponds to an entry Johann II made in his journal; namely, that after returning from his Walla Walla trip on April 14, he, Claus, and a man named Fritz Melzer traveled to Klickitat in Washington Territory to look at land, some 100 miles north and east of Middleton. While the land proved unsatisfactory ("many stones and cold winds"), he wrote, "...we bought a pony and two horses. After returning home, we spent some time breaking them, then we began hauling fence rails and such."[107]

What seems likely is that Claus and Johann had sent word to Hinrich that they wanted to buy horses, which they certainly needed to help clear their land of trees and stumps. While a relevant letter is not in the collection, it is quite possible that in this short note from late March, Hinrich wanted his brothers to know that he was sending them $2,000, two $500 bank drafts to each of them. This likely is the money he had written about sending in his February 9 letter and was intended to pay for the horses Claus and Johann were hoping to find.

---

[106] Letters of intent involved paying a small sum of money to record and publish your intention to buy land. It gave the signer an advantage, should they later decide to purchase the land. See *Hinrich*, p. 145 for more information.

[107] Johann II Schlichting, op. cit., p. 27 (also in *NWB*, p. 40).

Hinrich's letter—probably from late March—was short and to the point (from arrow): "...Very nice weather. Might sow soon. Received your last letter that it is wet, and that you want to buy young horses.
$500 $500 $500 $500
  Johann Claus sent"
Schlichting Letters Collection: 1878-03 maybe Hinrich S MN to Claus Joh II OR

On April 7 Hinrich dashed off another short letter to Claus and Johann II, noting that he had received their letters, including "the last one saying that you have received the money—$2,000—and that Johann is away to Walla Walla" (he would return to Middleton on April 14). Here an added comment about the $2,000: This was a large amount of money. That Hinrich could afford to send such sums to his brothers in Oregon seems surprising. It must be remembered, however, that in January of that year he had sold his first 160-acre farm in Minnesota (Parcel A) for $6,500, and that he was well established on his second farm (Parcel B). Fortunately, he could afford to send the needed cash to Oregon.

Hinrich ended this April 7 letter with a comment about the Minnesotans' forthcoming journey to Oregon: "As for when we will be coming, it has not yet been firmly set. It depends on what our situation is and will be."

In the chart of letters at the beginning of this chapter, the frequent exchange of letters between Oregon and Minnesota in 1878 is interrupted by a single letter from Peter Schlichting of Breitenwisch. It is dated April 16. In the Oste Dike area, the winter had been mild, but a strong storm in March had wreaked havoc, causing damage to the newly replaced roof of their farmhouse and leaving water standing in the polders. Fortunately, animals could be grazed on land that was already green with spring grass. He included news concerning neighbors the Americans would still know. He also added news about a neighbor named Johann Schlichting (from a different Schlichting family), whose house had burned but who was rebuilding. The details Peter added are interesting: "...the main room [is] 36 feet long, 15 feet high. The crossbeams in the roof are oak. Engelhard is building it for 2,600 Thaler. He has to finish the whole building. [In the meantime] the three [family members] are living with J. Schilling."

He also wrote about Anton Blank, beginning with a curious comment. Anton had moved out of the Schlichtings' old farmhouse in Neuland, citing as a reason that Johann I and his family didn't want him living there anymore. Peter's choice of words indicate that he doubted the claim. He then added the likely reason: "Anton has bought more wood. He wants to build a new house for himself." This matches news Anton himself had written in his Dec. 16, 1877, letter to Johann I (see Ch. 5). Peter wrote that Anton's bees had fared poorly in winter because he had neglected them, but that "All of mine made it through winter."

He also wrote a singular and curious sentence: "Just recently 300 horned cattle arrived in Hamburg from America." Peter provided no elaboration. He ended the letter with greetings from all the family: himself and his wife Maria, brother Diedrich, and sister Metta Hellwege and her family.

Back in America, on the 20th of April Johann II wrote to Hinrich,[108] describing what he had found on his travels: "I returned from Walla Walla on April 14. On the way back, I also went through part of Umatilla County, Oregon." From the descriptions that follow, he had been looking for more land that was suitable for farming. Overall, he felt that the country along the Snake River, farther north and east, was better than the land along the Columbia River. But even there the soil left much to be desired. He had heard that wooded land was still available around Dallas, Oregon, as well as near The Dalles on the Washington side of the Columbia River. Because the latter was closer to their farm, Johann wrote that "Claus and I are heading that way tomorrow, also because we've heard that horses are cheaper to buy there." But, he added, "As far as taking (i.e., buying) land is concerned, we probably will wait until all of you get here."

This letter was reprinted in *New World Beginnings* on p. 41. That translation does not differentiate between Dallas and The Dalles, but a photocopy of Johann II's original letter shows that he wrote each name distinctly, indicating two separate locations. Dallas is located west of Salem. In Johann's estimation, The Dalles was closer to the Middleton property; for that reason, and because horses were supposed to be cheaper to buy there as well, it would be their destination the next day. What came of that journey is not detailed in any letter we still have.

The rest of the letter consisted of routes for the Minnesotans to follow on their trip west. He enclosed a hand-drawn map showing possible routes from Omaha west. Johann's suggestion was for them to "...travel by train to Kelton on the Great Salt Lake and from there by stage or mail transport. You can purchase through tickets in Omaha." He added helpful suggestions regarding luggage: "Note that by mail [coach], luggage up to 50 lbs. in weight goes at no cost, whereas on the train the upper limit with no charge is 100 lbs. ... If you send your goods as freight, it would be best to ship them to Portland. Freight comes by that route anyway, and we still can't tell you another location." Thinking that they probably would travel by an overland route, Johann suggested that they meet in Walla Walla.

Which route the family took is not known, though a land route to Walla Walla, following Johann's suggestion, is certainly possible. During that summer of 1878, however, unrest involving the Bannock tribe erupted in violence, and travel there would have taken the family where fighting was taking place. This makes the family's choice for travel less certain. But whichever route they took, Johann II noted in his journal that they arrived safely in Middleton on June 20.[109]

---

[108] 1878-04-20 Johann II OR to Hinrich S MN.

[109] This topic is discussed in more detail in *Hinrich*, pp. 121ff.

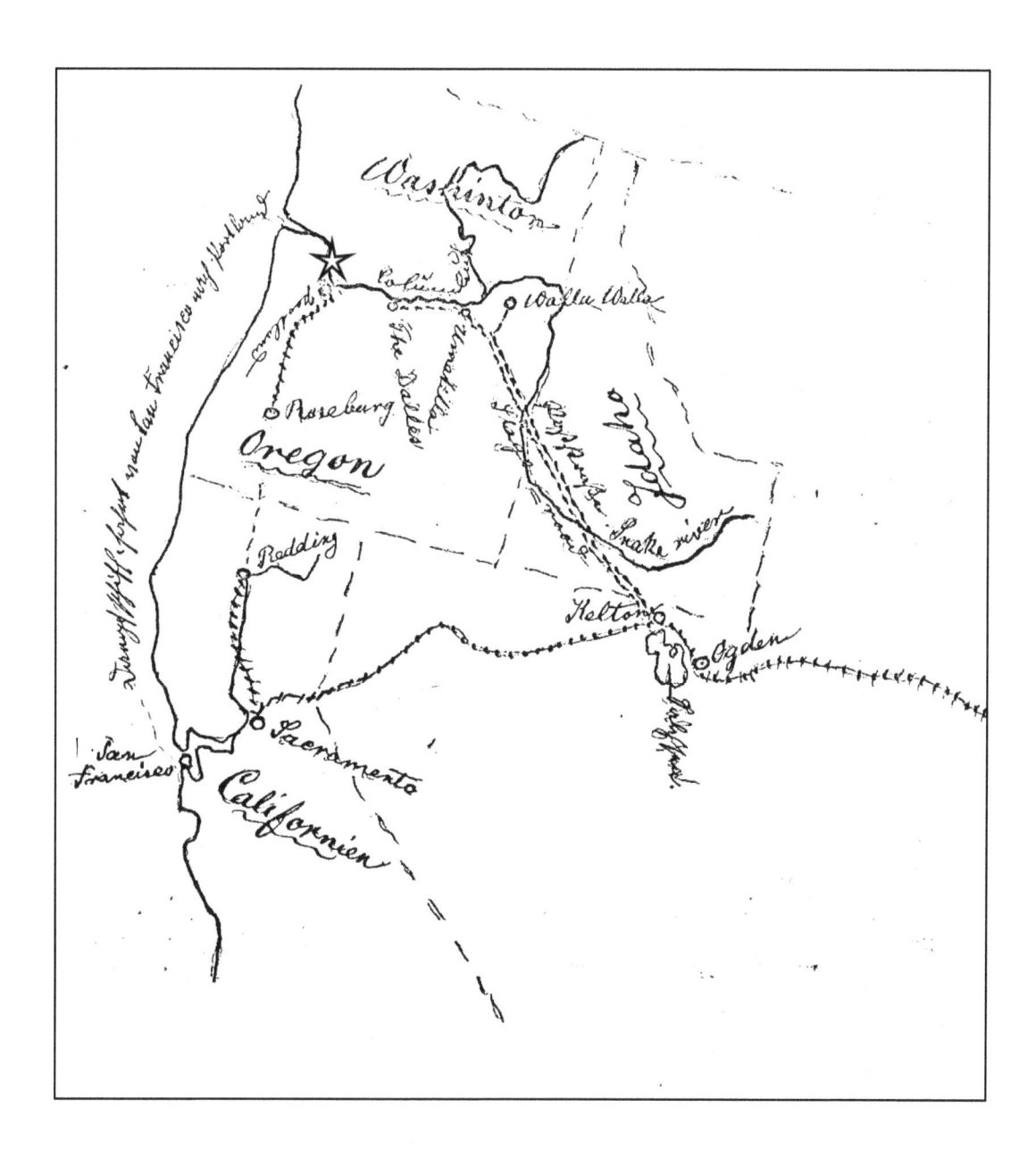

In his April 20, 1878, letter, Johann's hand-drawn map showed his Minnesota family three possible routes from Omaha (off the map to the right) to Portland (star):
   1) *by rail to Ogden and Kelton, Utah, then by mail coach through southwest Idaho and on to the Columbia River and The Dalles, with the option of Walla Walla as the destination;*
   2) *by rail to Sacramento, then north by rail through Redding Calif., and Roseburg, Ore., to Portland (he might have been uncertain whether the rail line was complete; hence the incomplete line in his sketch); or*
   3) *by rail to Sacramento, then by boat on the Sacramento River to San Francisco, and from San Francisco by ocean steamship to Portland. Which route the family chose is not known. Johann's own route in May 1877 had been Option 3.*

Schlichting Letters Collection, 1878-04-20 Joh II OR to Hinrich S MN.

A short letter from Hinrich on May 4 acknowledged receipt of Johann II's April 20th letter and ventured that the family would travel west as soon as possible.[110] He wrote, "We received your ('your' written in the plural) letter from Walla Walla and the journey, and that Johann has returned. I can't give a precise time [for our trip west]. I think we will be coming soon, but there is still a lot to organize…"

The long-anticipated trip west finally took place in June. The journey itself is not described in any documents we have, and as noted above, Johann's journal entry stated simply, "On June 20 F[ather] (V[ater]), H[inrich], R[ebecka] and M[inna Parsohn] arrived here from Minnesota."[111] Johann I was 68, Hinrich 41, and his sister Rebecka 25. Minna Parsohn, the young domestic worker who accompanied them, had been with the family in Minnesota since 1876. She continued living with them in Oregon.

Johann II provided no details about the route chosen by his family when they traveled in June 1878 from Minnesota to Oregon. In his journal page for 1878, he stated simply (in frame), "On June 20 V. H. R and M. arrived here from Minn." Johann II Schlichting Journal Part 3, p. 27.

In his journal, Johann II wrote that after the Minnesotans had arrived on June 20, he and Hinrich decided to venture east from Middleton to visit Umatilla County (where Johann had been in April) with the intention of finding more land to buy. He wrote, "We were ready to buy land (literally, "to take up land"). But then an Indian war began, and we had to delay the trip."[112] What he called an "Indian war" was the Bannock tribe's fight to preserve its ancestral lands. It lasted from June through August of that year.

Johann's description of what happened during this short period of time is packed into a few sparsely worded sentences in his journal: "…we had to postpone the trip. And then the time came when Hinrich had to leave again for Minnesota. Having considered the matter with Claus, [Hinrich] later wrote me out West and asked that I abandon that idea [of a land purchase] and return home, which I did. I was home again on August 2."[113] Two extant letters, from July 5 and July 22, help us to read between the lines of those meager facts and to reconstruct the sequence of events:

- Following a delay, Hinrich and Johann II left Middleton to travel to Umatilla County. This would have been very late June or very early July.
- July 5, Johann sent a brief note to Claus, informing him that he and Hinrich were in Milton, Oregon (today Milton-Freewater), and were seeking to avoid proximity to hostile Indians.

---

[110] 1878-05-04 Hinrich S MN to Claus Joh II S OR
[111] Johann II Schlichting op. cit., p. 27.
[112] *Ibid.*
[113] *Ibid.* Also, *Hinrich*, p. 124.

Merlin Schlichting ♦ 78

- Sometime after that, Hinrich returned to Middleton, leaving Johann to travel on his own.
- After returning to Middleton and reflecting on what he had seen and heard, Hinrich "considered the matter with Claus," "the matter" being whether to pursue a land purchase in the Umatilla area.
- July 22, Hinrich wrote (from Middleton) to Johann II, advising him to abandon his land search and to return to the farm.
- August 2, Johann arrived back in Middleton.

Johann's July 5, 1878, note to his brother Claus:
"At the moment we are in Milton, 10 miles south of Walla W[alla]. Just how close the Indians are I don't know, but they still seem far enough away. We will always stay far enough away from them."
~J. Schlichting

Schlichting Letters Collection: 1878-07-05 Joh II S OR to Claus S OR.

After Hinrich had returned alone to Middleton and conferred with Claus, he wrote to Johann II on July 22, apologizing that "my travels have taken longer than I thought they would."[114] He explained that he and Claus had spoken, and that they had decided to abandon seeking land in the Umatilla area. He listed the reasons behind the decision: "... [Claus and I] talked about it not being a good idea to be up there and claim land—Indians, no market, poor, white alkali soil and water, dust, dryness, wind, and illness. And the illness comes mostly from the dust and dryness. Claus is certain of that."

He wrote that he had heard about the dryness causing illness and even death in the areas around Walla Walla and Dayton, and he concluded by writing, "The best would be that you come back. Sell the wood the best you can. Claus will tell you everything he and I talked about and what we will do in the future." What was meant by "Sell the wood as best you can" is uncertain, but the long list of arguments against seeking land in that area was convincing enough that Johann agreed to return to Middleton. As he later wrote in his journal, he arrived there on August 2.

By the time he arrived back at the farm, however, Hinrich had left for Minnesota. In an undated letter to Claus, probably from late that summer of 1878, Hinrich acknowledged receiving a letter from Claus—not in our collection—stating that Johann II was back in Middleton.

Hinrich continued the letter by writing, "Father (Johann I) has to send [money] to Anton [Blank] and Diedrich [Schlichting] (Johann I's brother), $15 for each, or whatever Father thinks."[115] The money was to be paid from interest earned on Johann I's bank account. However, the interest would not be paid out until the new

---

[114] "1878-07-22 Hinrich S OR to Joh II S OR". Hinrich must have had an address where he could reach Johann.
[115] The German implies that Johann I felt an obligation to send money: *Vater der müsste doch wohl etwas an Anton und Diedrich x x x schicken.* That is, "Father really should send something..." The three x's probably indicate that the amount was not yet determined.

year, "...and that's probably too late," Hinrich wrote. He asked whether Claus or Johann II would send it. If they didn't want to or couldn't, they should let him know and he would send it. He concluded by adding a greeting from George and Teresa Burger, the couple who had bought Hinrich's first farm, Parcel A.

Johann II's final journal entry for 1878 was, "No work of significance was done [the rest of that year]. For a while, we looked about for farms to rent but that proved unsuccessful. So, we went about setting up the house and the barn as well as we could. We got ourselves a dog and a cat, 20 hens, and one cow with a calf."[116]

The last letter in this chapter is dated March 25, 1879,[117] and was written by Hinrich to Claus and Johann II. Hinrich made note of a March 7 letter they had sent him—not in our collection—and stated that he had sent two, $100 bank drafts in mid and late February. He was contemplating sending another $500 in early June but wrote that it wouldn't include money from their father.[118] He concluded with a reminder that his brothers should give him ample time to process their requests for money: "...it takes an awfully long time, so be sure to give me plenty of advance notice." This indicates both that the new property in Oregon required considerable infusions of cash, and that it was Hinrich who had ultimate control of the family's finances. His successful farming enterprise enabled him to maintain properties in two states, as well as to support the family.

A final word is added here as a reflection on the larger picture of the Schlichtings' migration west.

They traveled in June 1878, as the Bannock War was erupting in western Idaho and eastern Oregon.[119] Whether the travelers were aware of the imminent hostilities is not known. Like Johann II and Claus in 1877, they had to risk travel in a region where violence between U.S. troops and Native American tribes was flaring. It was a daunting challenge. David Schlichting wrote in *Hinrich*, "Between the 1876 Sioux battles in the Dakota Territory and the 1877 Nez Perce fiasco in the Northwest, it is surprising that the allure of Oregon still drew settlers, including the Schlichtings."[120]

However, reflecting on the family's firm decision to move west, and considering the overall attitude of white settlers and the American government toward Indigenous people in the United States, it is in fact not surprising that hostilities with Native Americans failed to deter westward expansion. Opportunities to settle "new" land—land that frequently had only recently been forcibly vacated by Indigenous tribes and communities—or to exploit the vast natural resources in the West, seemed unlimited. Unless hostilities threatened the settlers directly, Indians were for the most part invisible to them. They pursued their dreams as if native people didn't exist, and as if the land the settlers desired to occupy had never been inhabited. This would have been as true for our Schlichting forebears as for any other settlers.

At most, Native Americans would have posed an inconvenience to the pursuit of the settlers' goals. We need only read Johann II's letter of October 2, 1877 (see Ch. 5), in which he described his considerably altered route from Minnesota to Oregon in May of that year. The change was due to hostilities in eastern Oregon and western Idaho involving the Nez Perce people, who at

---

[116] Johann II Schlichting, op. cit., p. 27. Also reprinted in *New World Beginnings*, p. 40. The barn was likely a temporary shelter built for the animals. The last sentence originally was written above the top margin of p. 28a in the journal.
[117] 1879-03-25 Hinrich MN to Claus Joh II S OR.
[118] His father, Johann I, was in Oregon by then, but Hinrich was administering his father's finances, which remained based in Minnesota.
[119] For a description of the Bannock War, see *Hinrich*, p. 121.
[120] op. cit., p. 114.

that very time were involved in what for them was a life-or-death struggle to remain on their ancestral lands.

The hostilities forced Johann's travel plans to change. Rather than traveling overland directly to Oregon, Johann had to "detour" to San Francisco and then sail by steamship north to Portland. It was an inconvenience to be sure, but it did not deter him from his goal, nor, we may assume, did the reasons behind the hostilities or the importance of finding a just settlement with the Nez Perce cause him to have second thoughts. The pursuit of finding land to buy trumped all other considerations. Numerous letters in our collection attest to that.

A year later, in July of 1878, during what was called the Bannock War, Johann and Hinrich ventured out from Middleton in search of land, this time traveling to Umatilla County in eastern Oregon. As described above, this was the trip they had planned to take but then postponed because of the hostilities. After a brief delay, they started the journey. While underway, Johann sent the July 5 note to Claus, in which he assured his brother, "...I don't know exactly how close the Indians are, but they are still quite some distance. We will always stay far enough away from them."[121]

This single-mindedness of purpose, to the exclusion of all other considerations, only underscores what is written above. The plight of the Indigenous people and their doomed fight to retain their ancestral land—land that was also a primary source of their food—posed nothing more than an inconvenience to those hungry to buy land. Despite the danger of being caught up in armed hostilities, our family's pursuit of finding more land to buy did not end until Hinrich wrote Johann a few weeks later, via Claus, to give up the search.

---

[121] 1878-07-05 Johann II S OR to Claus S OR.

CHAPTER 7

1880

A Notable Death and Two Weddings, Transitions

Date	Source	Writer in Germany / Recipient	Writer in U.S. / Recipient	Comments
1880 maybe (year uncertain)	original		Hinrich S, Minn, to Claus S, Ore.	Undated. Hinrich also had written to Rebecka. He had concerns about the Middleton mortgage and Rebecka's welfare. Advised caution on growing hops.
1880 before July	photocopy	Peter S, Breitenwisch, to Claus, Joh II S, Ore.		Undated but written prior to July, served as letter of introduction to Diedrich Schlichting of Grossenwoerden, Peter's nephew by marriage
1880 January 9, Johann I Schlichting died, in Oregon, aged 69.					
1880 Jan 18	photocopy	Peter S, Brtnw, and Metta Hellwege, Kleinwoerden to Johann I S, Ore.		Short letter by Metta, recently widowed. Longer letter by Peter with info. about Metta's situation. Relayed comments by Anton Blank re. his plans to build a house.
1880 Feb 15	photocopy	Peter S, Brtnw, to Johann I S, Ore.		Peter would send seeds to Ore. Poor harvest followed by hard winter, some famine. Re. Anton Blank: he had bought land, would build soon.
1880 July 7	photocopy	Peter S, Brtnw, to Relatives in Ore.		Had received word of Johann I's death. Metta's daughter had died. Anton Blank moved into new house, news about him. Sent update re. brother Diedrich's children. Cold spring & a late frost, then rainy summer; harvest would be poor.
1880 July 6, Hinrich Schlichting and Caroline Truebenbach married, St. John Lutheran Church in Jacksonville, Minn.					
1880 July 10, Rebecka Schlichting and Thomas Matthiesen married, St. Paul Lutheran Church in Middleton (Sherwood), Ore.					
1880 July 11	photocopy	Diedrich S, Grossenwoerden, to Claus & Joh II S., Ore.		He remembered both Rebecka and Anton. Expressed desire to emigrate, asked C&J's advice on numerous related matters.
1880 late summer or early fall, Hinrich and Caroline moved to Dakota Territory, spent winter there.					
1880 Dec. 9, in two parts	original		Hinrich S., Dakota Territory, to Claus & Joh II S, Ore.	First part: Farming there was hard. Concerns re. Rebecka's & Claus' health. Would write later re. Dakota Territory. Second part: Described fast growth of area following laying of rail lines. Compared Dakota farming to that in Lake City, Minn.

After the flurry of letter exchanges between the Schlichtings in Oregon and in Minnesota during 1877 and 1878, by 1880 the pace had slowed considerably. The most likely reasons for this are:

- First and most obvious, letters that were written might since have been lost. Beyond that,
- In Oregon, the family was working to improve the farm they had bought. This included clearing more trees, stumps, and brush (slash) from the land and sowing first crops. The family also began construction of a barn and thought about building a permanent house (at first, they all lived in the small cabin that was already on the land when they bought it).[122]
- Claus and Johann II also were involved in the formation of St. Paul Lutheran Church in Middleton; they are credited with the construction of the first sanctuary.[123]
- In Minnesota, Hinrich continued developing his farm (Parcel B). In April 1880 he purchased another 40 acres (Parcel C), bringing his holdings to more than 200 acres.
- Hinrich also was involved in the formation of St. John Lutheran Church in Jacksonville and was a leader in both construction and financial support of the church.[124]

From June 1878 forward, all family members except Hinrich were living on the new property in Oregon. At first, they lived in the small cabin that already stood south of the Tualatin River. "All" included father, Johann I (67), daughter Rebecka (25), sons Claus (38) and Johann II (34), and their domestic helper Minna Parsohn, a teenage girl who had come with them from Minnesota. Quarters were cramped, to say the least.

Johann II's journal reveals that from winter 1878/79 into spring, they had hired workers to help clear land. A first seeding of oats did not provide grain—it was sown too late—but it was harvested as fodder for their animals. Potatoes produced a good yield. In summer 1879 more workers were hired for clearing, and the first section of a barn was built. In fall 1879 construction was started on a new house, located close to the new barn, farther away from the river and on higher ground. It should be remembered that Claus and Johann II were both accomplished carpenters, and their skill resulted in carefully constructed, solid buildings. The barn they built remains standing to this day. By spring 1880 the house kitchen was sufficiently completed to be used, and in June the family moved into the house altogether.[125]

In his journal, Johann II noted that during late 1879, their father Johann I became ill with what then was called dropsy, today described as edema. The condition worsened, leaving him increasingly weak, until he died on January 9, 1880, at the age of 69.

In a lifespan of nearly 70 years (1810-1880), Johann I had experienced huge changes, especially during the last 14 years of his life. After his wife Elisabeth died in 1866 at their Neuland, Oste Dike farm in Germany, he had seen his three oldest sons emigrate to America. Then in 1869, having sold his small farm, he and his two youngest children, Rebecka and Anton, followed them (guided by son Hinrich) by ship to New York and then by rail to a reunion of all in Milwaukee. That same fall he journeyed with Hinrich, Rebecka, and Anton into southeastern Minnesota, where

---

[122] Johann II Schlichting, op. cit., p. 29. See also, *Hinrich*, pp. 181-182.
[123] Johann II devoted two full pages in his journal (pp. 28a-28b) to describing the congregation's founding and first years.
[124] A narrative of the church's founding and Hinrich's involvement can be found in *Hinrich*, pp. 116-120. Also, Rebecka's letter to Claus and Johann II from February 1878 stated that lumber and bricks had been delivered for building the church, and that construction would start soon, weather permitting (1878-02-08 Rebecka S MN to Claus Joh II S OR). See Ch. 6.
[125] Johann II Schlichting, op. cit., p. 29.

they began to farm, purchasing their first property in June of 1870.

In September the following year, his youngest son Anton became ill and died at age 17. This threw the 61-year-old man into despair so great that he declared he wanted to return to Germany. But when given the opportunity, and the money, to do it—this was discussed in Chapter 5—he decided to remain in America with his other children. Within a few years, he was persuaded to move to Oregon, where sons Johann II and Claus had relocated and were trying to convert recent forest land into farmland. In June of 1878 at nearly 68 years of age, he, daughter Rebecka, and the teenage girl Minna Parsohn made the long journey from Minnesota to Oregon, guided once again by oldest son Hinrich.

His death marked the end of a remarkable life. He was buried in the cemetery of St. Paul Lutheran Church in Middleton (later Sherwood), Oregon. A monument still marks the gravesite.

The grave marker of Johann I Schlichting, at the St. Paul Lutheran Church Cemetery, Sherwood, Oregon. The inscription reads:
"Here rests in God
our beloved father
Johann Schlichting
born
20 August 1810
died
9 January 1880."
The text of Revelation 14:13 is inscribed beneath:
"Blessed are the dead who from now on die in the Lord."

As noted, Hinrich had resumed farming near Lake City, Minnesota. In late April 1880, he purchased another 40 acres of land (Parcel C), located about a mile-and-a-half east of Parcel B where he lived. Together with a hired man and a female domestic helper, Hinrich was now farming more than 200 acres of land.

As a result of his efforts and the fertility of the prairie soil, he was able to earn sufficient income to finance not only his own farm but also the property in Oregon, where an influx of capital was always needed. This is borne out by frequent references in letters to significant sums of money sent westward. In the booklet *New World Beginnings*, John August Schlichting (Hinrich's oldest son) later wrote: "The [Oregon] land selected was and is one of the choicest in the valley. Early crops were poor for a number of reasons. The land had to learn how to breathe after centuries of heavy forest...mingled with fern [that] had grown upon it. Preparing the soil was another lesson to be learned. This was quite different from Minnesota."[126]

Weddings in Oregon and Minnesota

In July 1880 two important family events took place. In Oregon, Rebecka Schlichting married Thomas Matthiesen on July 10. The couple resided at Thomas' nearby farm from then on. In Minnesota, Hinrich married Caroline Truebenbach on July 6 at the Lutheran church in Jacksonville. Theirs was the first wedding to be held in the new church. Hinrich and Caroline remained on the Jacksonville farm for a few months, but in late summer or early fall they packed up and headed west for the Dakota Territory. One letter of Hinrich to his Oregon brothers, posted from Big Stone City, Dakota Territory, and dated December 9, 1880, remains in our collection. It will be discussed below.[127]

Hinrich Schlichting and Caroline Truebenbach were married on July 6, 1880, at St. John Lutheran Church in Jacksonville, Minnesota.
Source: David Schlichting collection

---

[126] *New World Beginnings for the Schlichting Family*, p. 44.

[127] The time spent in Dakota Territory and acquisition of land there is discussed in detail in *Hinrich*, Chapter 11.

Undated 1880 Letter of Hinrich, Minnesota, to his brother Claus, Oregon

This undated letter has been placed into the 1880 timeframe.[128] It is an original in the collection, but it is in fragile condition, with parts of the paper torn and disintegrated. While it could have been written later than 1880, its contents address a matter that had been of concern to Hinrich for some time (as it had to his father). Their sister Rebecka had loaned Johann II and Claus $1,500 for the purchase of property in Oregon. This loan was to be repaid, but Johann II or Claus were never able to do that. They only managed to make annual interest payments.[129]

The following is a speculative yet feasible interpretation of Hinrich's letter. He began by stating, "We also wrote to Rebeka [sic]." This indicates that Rebecka was no longer living with her brothers but had married and was living with her husband Thomas Matthiesen on a nearby farm—in other words, after July 11, 1880. Hinrich then wrote, "We can arrange that with the mortgage, but probably not until spring. Meanwhile you can write me whether ... you also ... have to pay there. Otherwise, we will have to find another way. By then you will have learned..." The ellipses indicate places where the paper has disintegrated and text is missing.

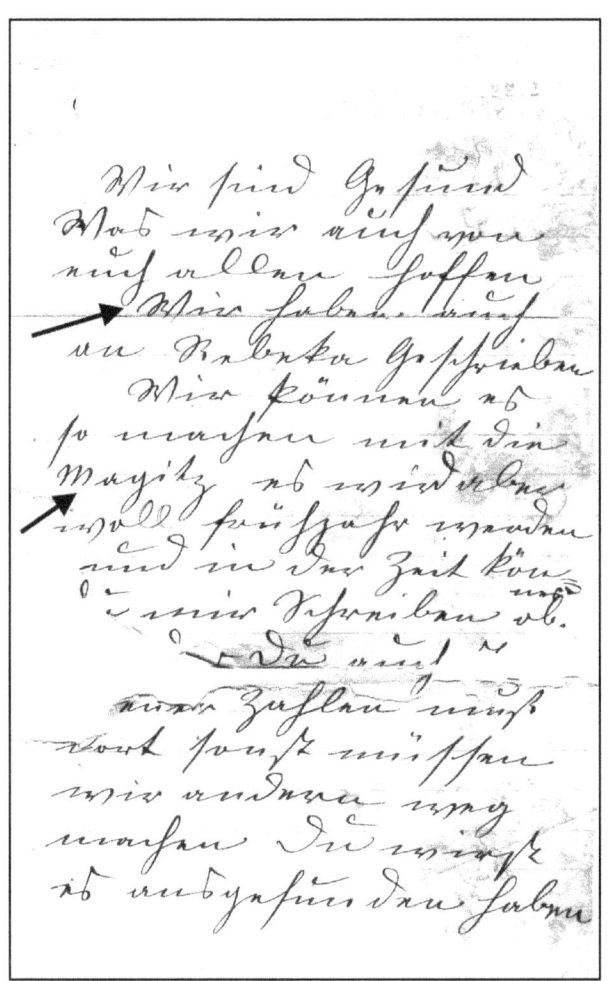

This letter from Hinrich was not dated and could have been written anytime between 1880 and 1883. It likely was intended for his brother Claus (it was found in the same envelope as an 1882 letter he wrote specifically to Claus). The letter expressed Hinrich's concerns that money loaned by Rebecka for the purchase of the Oregon farm should be repaid her.

He wrote (from top arrow), "We also wrote to Rebeka [sic]. We can arrange that with a mortgage, but probably not until spring. Meanwhile, you can write me whether ... you also ... have to pay there. Otherwise, we will have to find another way. By then you will have learned..." Ellipses indicate tears in the paper resulting in missing words.

Schlichting Letters Collection: 1880 maybe – Hinrich S MN to Claus S OR.

---

[128] "1880 maybe – Hinrich S MN to Claus S OR."
[129] See *Hinrich*, p. 120 for further explanation.

The Emigrant Letters ♦ 87

For "mortgage" Hinrich used the peculiar word "Magitz" (lower arrow in image), which is likely his phonetic transliteration of "mortgage" into a nonexistent "German" word. Hinrich frequently used invented German words in his letters, with interesting results.[130]

On a second page, Hinrich continued, "Is everything all right with Rebecka? Let's see to it that we keep things straight."[131] The last words in his letter were, "Remember to write about the mortgage." Unfortunately, we have no other letters to provide explanation or reports of any developments. And as it turned out, the repayment of that and other debts was a dilemma that would not be resolved by either Claus or Johann II. This will be discussed in a later chapter.

One more comment about this short letter. It would seem Claus had written to Hinrich about the possibility of growing hops on the Oregon property. This was a matter with which Hinrich was well acquainted from early days in Minnesota, and his response was curt: "Be careful with hops. There's a lot of work to [growing them]."[132]

Undated 1880 Letter of Peter Schlichting, Breitenwisch, to Claus and Johann II Schlichting, Oregon

Another undated letter in the chart was written in the first part of 1880 by Peter Schlichting of Breitenwisch. It served as a letter of introduction for his nephew by marriage, a young man named Diedrich Schlichting, who lived with his parents and brother in the town of Grossenwoerden. Despite having the same family name, this Diedrich was part of a different Schlichting family. Peter wrote about the young man's situation and his desire to emigrate to America. Diedrich's intention was to write to Claus and Johann II to introduce himself. He did in fact write, on July 11. The letter will be discussed below.

Three 1880 Letters of Peter Schlichting, Breitenwisch, to the Oregon family

Three more letters from Peter Schlichting in Germany also appear in our chart: from January 18, February 15, and July 7. As was noted above, Peter's brother Johann I died in Oregon on January 9, 1880. When Peter sent the first two of these letters, he was not aware of his brother's death. Not until the July letter did he acknowledge having received that information. The letters and their primary contents are described here:
- January 18—Both Peter and his sister Metta Hellwege wrote segments of this letter. Assuming that she was writing to her brother, Johann I, Metta began by informing him that her husband, Johann Andreas Hellwege, had died on September 8. "Like you, I am now widowed," she wrote. She added comments about (mostly unfavorable) changes that had come to her small village of Kleinwoerden.[133] Peter continued the letter where she left off, commenting on Metta's situation: "...she wants to rent out a room and some land. Selling the cow and doing extra weaving will raise more money."

He included word about Johann I's brother-in-law Anton Blank, recalling a conversation Anton had had with him and about how Anton had arrived at the decision to build: "I can't live at my sister's[134] because that room

---

[130] A word Hinrich often used was *Dref*, by which he meant "draft," as in a bank draft.
[131] Hinrich wrote *stret*, another transliteration, this time of the English word "straight."
[132] Hinrich's oldest son, John August Schlichting, wrote in his memoir about growing hops in Minnesota: *As I Remember*, pp. 20-21.

[133] Kleinwoerden is located on the west bank of the Oste River, directly across from Neuland Oste Dike. See Google Maps coordinates 53.66000, 9.27444.
[134] Anton's older sister was Margaretha (Blank) Spreckels, who lived in the town of Hammah, a few miles east of Neuland. See Google Maps, coordinates 53.618214, 9.375088.

is not fit for human habitation. It's not much different at Bartholt König's. The house leaks on the north side...For that reason, I am going to build myself a small house. Then I can live on the south side. And I can earn something using my boat for fishing (on the Oste River). I can build the house as time allows." Peter noted that Anton had received money from the Oregon Schlichtings and would welcome more, though Peter himself did not intend to contribute. He ended by relaying that his brother Diedrich was well, also that due to the prohibitive cost, the package he was planning to send would be a small one.

- February 15—Still unaware of Johann I's death in January, Peter began this letter by describing seeds he was sending to him: large beans from a neighbor, C. Koppelmann, and a smaller seed from the Oste Dike that he himself had harvested. The list continued and included "small, rough peas, yellow and green sugar peas. I'd also like to give you a small, coarse Egyptian rye."

He ended with the news that Anton Blank had bought land from the Horn Mill owner Schroeder to build his house, about four acres in size, close to the gristmill and along the river. During the previous fall, he had built up a berm, on which the house would be built.[135] Anton already had the wood and would be getting stones for the foundation. He had secured the services of a carpenter named Thumann, while E. Neuland would build cabinetry. He was hoping to get by on his budget.

A photo of the gristmill in the town of Hemmoor, not far from Neuland. Located immediately behind the dike (foreground), this wind-powered gristmill operated between 1845 and 1993. In appearance it would have been very similar to the mill in Neuland-Horn, where Anton Blank was employed for several years as lock keeper. After the watermill was converted into a gristmill, Anton was no longer employed but continued to live in Neuland-Horn, on land next to the dike that he bought in 1880 from the mill's owner. The Neuland-Horn mill was torn down in the 1960s.

- July 7—Peter acknowledged receiving news of Johann I's death in an April 9 letter from Oregon —not in our collection. He wrote that sister Metta's daughter, Katharina, had died the previous month at eight years of age. A five-year-old son, Johann, was healthy.[136] Peter added new information about Anton Blank: "[He] moved into his new house shortly after Easter. His close neighbor is Bartels, the miller (as I mentioned earlier, the Peters' watermill is [now] set up as a gristmill for grain) ... Anton still fishes. He has a boat which is indispensable for that. He keeps sheep on a meadow he rents next to the house.

---

[135] In the low-lying Oste Dike area, houses were often built on berms of built-up soil for protection from flooding.

[136] Church records show that Johann Hellwege grew to adulthood in Kleinwoerden, married, and raised three daughters. He died there in 1951 (from the parish records of Hechthausen).

His house is 30 feet long and 18 feet wide, built from sawn fir wood. It is a seemly and attractive house." Peter noted how neighbors had helped Anton by delivering building supplies and other material. He also included an update of his brother Diedrich's family. Weather had been wet, causing hay to rot in the fields, while a late spring frost had caused a poor bloom in fruit trees. Neither honey nor fruit would be plentiful at harvest.

The site of the house Anton Blank had built in 1880 near the Horn Mill in Neuland Oste Dike along the inner dike of the river. The windmill stood about 75 yards to the right of the photo. Anton's wood-built house stood on the low elevation just right of the small bridge (arrow). Anton supported himself by fishing on the river and kept a small number of sheep, which he grazed along the dike. While he was able, he also worked at various jobs in the nearby area. The house was torn down after Anton's death in 1916.

July 11, 1880, Letter of Diedrich Schlichting, Grossenwoerden, to Claus and Johann II Schlichting, Oregon

The last two letters we have from 1880 are of quite different character. Peter had written earlier in the year to introduce a young man named Diedrich Schlichting, his nephew by marriage but not part of our Schlichting family. This Diedrich wrote to Claus and Johann II in Oregon on July 11, primarily to ask their opinions on several matters touching on his hoped-for emigration to America the following spring. He wrote that his primary reason to emigrate was economic—falling wage levels. In his early to mid-twenties, he had completed his compulsory military service and was thus free to leave the country. He mentioned that he had been confirmed with Rebecka Schlichting and had known her younger brother Anton in school.

Diedrich asked several questions that reveal not only curiosity but also perceptions, or misperceptions, of life in America: How much does a worker earn there? How much does is cost to travel by train? What sorts of things do I need to bring? If too many people come there, will wages fall? What's the best way to get to you, via San Francisco? And finally, "Would it be good for me to learn English this winter, or is that unnecessary?" It is unlikely that Diedrich followed through on his hopes to go to America. A letter of Peter Schlichting from June 1881 indicated that his plans did not meet with his mother's approval (see Ch. 8).

December 9, 1880, Letter of Hinrich Schlichting, Minnesota, to brothers Claus and Johann II, Oregon

The final letter from this year was written December 9 by Hinrich to his Oregon brothers—addressed to Johann II but clearly intended for both him and Claus. It was sent from Big Stone City in Dakota Territory (now South Dakota). A thorough discussion of Hinrich and Caroline's sojourn in that region can be read in *Hinrich*, in Chapter 11. They arrived there in late summer or early fall 1880, not long after their wedding. Thus, by December 9 when Hinrich wrote the letter, they had been there no more than a few months. Hinrich bought a parcel of land by the process called preemption. Caroline was pregnant with their first child.

Where they lived that winter is not entirely clear, but with the envelope postmarked in Big Stone City the same day Hinrich wrote it, December 9, it seems likely that they chose to spend the winter there.[137] As noted in *Hinrich*, they could not have chosen a worse winter to be there, seeing as the winter of 1880/81 was one of historic intensity, beginning with an early blizzard in October and lasting well into the following May. At the earliest opportunity in spring, they left and returned to the Lake City farm, in enough time for a daughter they named Elizabeth (Hinrich's late mother's name) to be born on June 29. Hinrich himself never farmed the Dakota land he bought, though he retained ownership until 1899, renting it out for crop farming in the intervening years.

---

[137] Anecdotal evidence in *New World Beginnings* (p. 11) suggests that they spent the winter in a sod house, but that is questionable. Other possibilities for their housing that winter are discussed in *Hinrich* on pp. 152-153.

The letter Hinrich wrote from Dakota Territory on December 9, 1880, was postmarked the same day in Big Stone City, now in South Dakota.

In this letter, Hinrich went to some lengths to describe what he had discovered in Dakota Territory: "Farming here is likely more work than for you [in Oregon].[138] I am gradually learning more about this area." Hinrich then continued his letter on two longer pages, describing how fast the area was growing, with people claiming land as fast as the railroad company could lay sections of track, and with new towns springing up along the tracks. He mentioned that crops grew well, but he also had heard how grasshoppers could wreak great havoc (though their dead bodies also served as fertilizer). And there was the climate to consider: "...in a raw climate such as this (much worse than Lake City), there must be large barns—barns and houses, before anything else is done."

Even though by December of that year the worst winter in memory was already raging, Hinrich wrote about it as if it hadn't affected him or Caroline personally: "There are supposedly four to five big snowstorms in the winter, but not all that much snow, because it always gets quite cold (19 degrees below zero). Sleighs don't work very well because the snow always drifts—not the way it is in Lake City. You can reckon with four inches of snow." The closing lines of the letter, however, offer a less than enthusiastic endorsement of the area: "Corn doesn't grow as well here as in Lake City. There are a lot of mosquitoes, and also flies, which are very unhealthy. Bugs are always dirty customers, also here."[139]

---

[138] This is a curious comment, given the amount of work needed to transform the Oregon property into arable farmland, though perhaps Hinrich had something else in mind when he wrote it.

[139] "dirty customers" approximates the derogatory word Hinrich wrote, *Schmutzlümmels*. It could also be translated "dirty bums," or "miserable characters," or worse.

CHAPTER 8

1881-1885

Oregon Ventures: An Untimely Death, Changes for the Oste Dike Family

Date	Source	Writer in Germany / Recipient	Writer in U.S. / Recipient	Comments
1881 June 9	original	Peter Schlichting, Breitenwisch, to Claus & Joh II Schlichting, Ore.		Asked about Rebecka and Hinrich. Diedrich Schlichting emigration; others want to emigrate. Wet fall caused flooding, slowing fall planting. Train line between Harburg and Stade now completed. Gave the picture to Anton B. Claus Jarck was living in their Neuland house. Metta doing all right. Cited costs for various products. Requested seeds.
1881 Nov 19	original		Hinrich S, Minn., to Claus & Joh II S, Ore.	Note 1: Sent $500 on 11/16. Would send more in late Nov. Asked for info. re. the property. Note 2: Had sent money several times, would send more in Jan. Sent letter from Klein.
1882 Apr 27	photocopy	Peter Schlichting, Brtnw, to Claus S., Ore.		Peter was caring for his brother Diedrich, who was unwell. Anton Blank's situation. Neighborhood, crops, and livestock news. Engelschoff planning to build a steam engine to pump water from polders.
1882 May 18	original		Unknown person in Portland Ore., to Claus S, Ore.	Described a hotel in Portland for possible purchase, including sketch of layout.
1882 July 1	original		HC Bronco, Walla Walla, Wash., to Claus S, Portland, Ore.	A postcard from H.C. Bronco of Lake City, Minn. but mailed from Walla Walla. Asked that Claus send him word, should H.C.'s lost wallet be found.
1882 Sept 20	original		Hinrich S, Minn., to Joh II S, Ore.	Wrote regarding harvest (possibly) and fall farm work. Asked that Claus & Rebecka read it, too.
1882 Nov 10	original		Hinrich S, Minn. to Claus Joh II S, Ore.	Commented about Portland businesses. Land prices, use of Rebecka's money. Bought a binder for harvesting. Crop, livestock report.

Feb. 7, 1883, Diedrich Schlichting of Breitenwisch died, aged 68 (brother of Johann I, Peter, and Metta).

Date	Source	Writer in Germany / Recipient	Writer in U.S. / Recipient	Comments
1883 Feb 24	original	Peter Schlichting, Brtnw, to Claus & Johann II, Rebecka M. and husband, Ore.		His brother Diedrich had died on Feb. 7. Peter's wife Maria, sister Metta, and Anton Blank all well. Horst parish to lay out new cemetery.

June 5, 1883, Johann II Schlichting died in Portland, Oregon, aged 39.

| 1885 Feb 17 | original | Peter Schlichting, Brtnw, to Claus S & family, Ore. | | Greetings from everyone. Wrote about J. Blanck in Götzdorf. Anton Blank was well but didn't receive the best care. Neighborhood news: Shoemaker Horreis was living in their former Neuland house. Learned that brother Diedrich's son Johann had emigrated to America in 1882, sent for wife & child later. End of letter missing. |

The first letter in this part of the collection was written on June 9, 1881, by Peter Schlichting in Breitenwisch. Just as he had communicated over the years with his brother Johann I in America, Peter now continued to send letters to his niece Rebecka and nephews Claus and Johann II in Oregon. In one of his letters, Peter stated that he had heard from Hinrich in Minnesota as well. But if the number of letters from these years in the collection is an indication, it seems he no longer wrote as often as he had earlier.

Peter's June 9th letter touched on many topics:

• He had received a letter from Rebecka, informing him of her marriage. He asked whether Hinrich was still farming in Minnesota. This indicates Peter had not had recent contact with him (Hinrich and Caroline had spent the winter months of 1880/81 in Dakota Territory—see Chapter 7).

• He asked whether the bean and pea seeds he sent had grown (in a Feb. 15, 1880 letter, he had written that he was sending them). At the end of the letter, he also asked them to send him seeds they thought he might be able to grow.

• He wrote about Diedrich Schlichting, the young man from Grossenwoerden[140] who had written Claus and Johann II the previous July to ask questions about emigration to the U.S. and a possible visit to them in Oregon. Peter wrote that the young man's plan had been stopped in its tracks: "Nothing will come of Diedrich Schlichting's trip to you. His mother doesn't want him to leave. It was his father who had okayed it."[141]

• Wet weather the previous fall had hindered fall seeding. A wet winter followed which caused flooding. Then it had been very cold early in 1881.

• The villages of Neuland and Engelschoff intended to build a steam mill to pump water standing in the polders—due to winter storms—into the Oste River. He thought they could complete the project before winter set in again.

• The railroad line was now complete between the county seat of Stade and Harburg (a suburb of Hamburg) on the Elbe River. The line is still in operation and runs through Himmelpforten, a few miles south of Breitenwisch.

• He had given a picture the American family had sent to their uncle, Anton Blank.

• Between weaving, raising some crops to sell, and keeping livestock, his widowed sister Metta Hellwege was just managing to get by.

• Peter reported higher costs for wheat and rye flour, coffee beans, and tobacco.

On November 19 Hinrich sent a scribbled note to Claus and Johann II with details about transfers of money in the form of bank drafts. The letter is copied and translated here:

---

[140] Grossenwoerden is a village just north of Neuland Oste Dike. See Google Maps coordinates 53.67952, 9.23018.

[141] See Ch. 7 regarding Diedrich Schlichting's July 7, 1880, letter.

Merlin Schlichting • 94

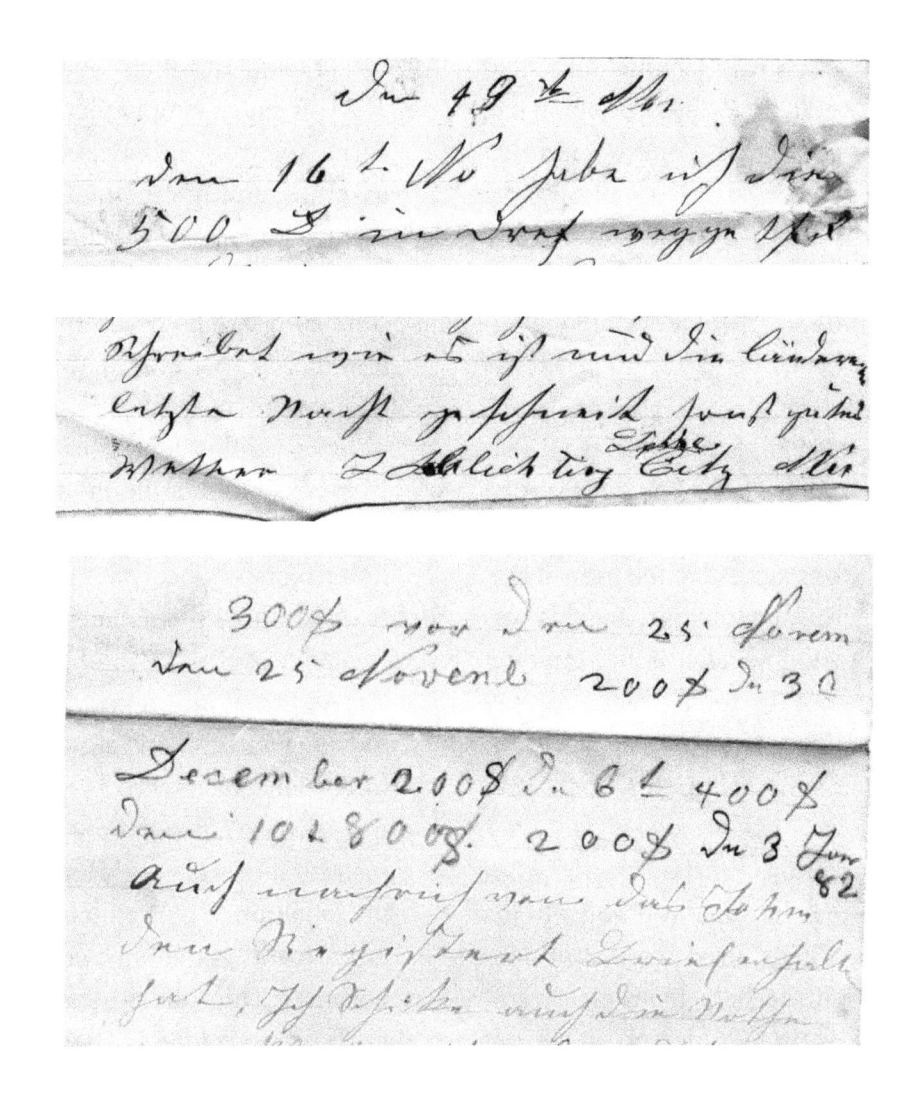

Hinrich's Nov. 19, (1881), scribbled note to Claus and Johann II is a challenge to read. He wrote:

"On Nov. 16th I sent off the $500 as a [bank] draft ... Write me how things stand with the property (die ländereien). Last night it snowed; otherwise, we are having good weather."

On the second page he outlined how he planned to send further bank drafts. With words and punctuation added for clarity, it reads:

"I'll send $300 before November 25, then $200 on November 25. On the 3rd of December, $200, on December 6, $400, and $800 on the 10th. On Jan. 3, [18]82, $200."

Schlichting Letters Collection, 1881-11-19 Hinrich S MN to Claus Joh II S OR

Altogether what Hinrich was sending amounted to an impressive $2,600. Given such a sum, it can be appreciated that Hinrich's Minnesota farming enterprise had been successful. Not only was he able to run his own farm—by that date in 1881 he farmed more than 200 acres—and to support a now growing family; he still had enough available capital to send such sums of money to his brothers in Oregon.

A logical question also follows. By 1881, how could the operation of the Oregon farm be so costly and need so much of a "subsidy" from Hinrich? Part of the answer is that the farm at that time still was not generating income, and this was due in large part to the necessary and ongoing clearing of remnants of the forests that once had covered the area. Comments to that effect by John August Schlichting, Hinrich's son, were noted in Chapter 6.

In addition, conditions on the Oregon property required outside help. Johann II noted in his journal that he and Claus hired workers in two years, 1879 and 1880, to help them clear remnants ("slash") left from logging and to dig out the stumps of mature trees that had been logged, a process called grubbing. Even though they sowed crops on the land they had cleared, the yields were minimal.[142] What they were learning was that this landscape, and this soil, was vastly different from the largely treeless but very fertile prairie soil they had known in Minnesota. The Oregon land would not become profitable as farmland for years.

Johann II's final journal entry was from 1881. It stated simply that he moved "to do some carpenter work in Portland on June 17."[143] The assumption might be that he did so to create an income stream. But events then took a surprising turn. Later in 1881 he and Claus invested in Europe House, a hotel in downtown Portland. And less than a year after that, Johann II bought into another downtown business, the Portland Restaurant. To do this Johann had to borrow money.[144] It is possible that the money Hinrich sent at the end of 1881 and the beginning of 1882—see his letter of Nov. 19, 1881, above—was connected to these investments and was not just for farm-related costs."[145]

A short note—a postcard actually—was sent to Claus on July 1, 1882; it was addressed to him in Portland, at "B Street between first & Second." In the book *Hinrich* on page 183, there is an illustration of a Europe House business card, with the notation, "C. Schlichting & Bro., Proprietors." It shows the same address as the one on the postcard. Thus, the postcard was sent to Claus at his business address. The postcard was sent by a man named H.C. Bronco, from Lake City, Minnesota, who apparently had stayed at the Europe House. On the way to the boat landing (on the Willamette River just a few blocks away) Bronco lost his pocketbook. On his way back east, he wrote from Walla Walla to ask Claus to notify him if the pocketbook was found.

---

[142] Johann II Schlichting, op. cit. p. 29.
[143] Johann II Schlichting, op. cit., p. 30.
[144] See *Hinrich*, pp. 182-184, for a discussion of this topic.
[145] See, *Hinrich*, pp. 182-185, and p. 191.

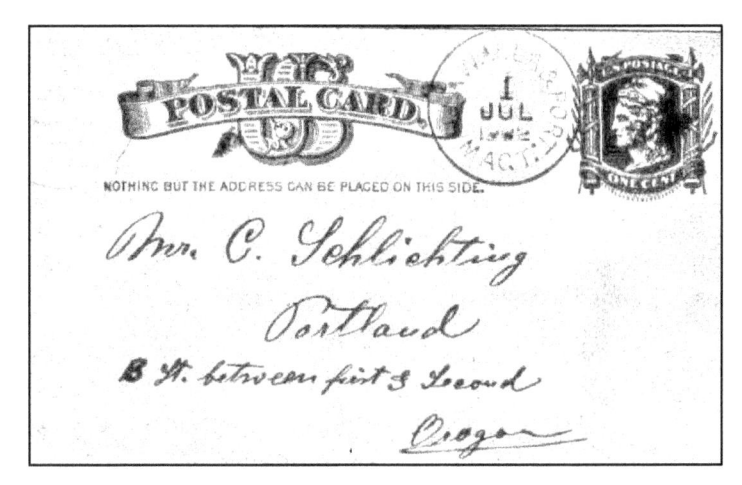

The postcard sent by HC Bronco to Claus was addressed to him at the Europe House hotel: "B St. between first & Second."
Schlichting Letters Collection: 1882-07-01 HC Bronco to Claus S Portland OR

Claus and Johann's inquiries into further investments continued. In a letter from May 18, 1882, an unnamed person wrote from Portland to Claus on the farm in Middleton. Apparently, Claus had engaged this person to look at another hotel in downtown Portland, the Eagle Hotel, and to report on its potential. The letter writer had visited the hotel and then sent Claus his evaluation, which included a sketch of the floorplan.

Overall, the evaluation was not positive: "[The hotel] has 55 single and 16 double beds. Not all are twin beds. Some rooms are very pleasant, but more than half have no outside windows, which means they can't be aired out very well." The main floor didn't impress him either: "There are no sleeping rooms there. Dining and sitting rooms are too large, although bright...The baggage room is inconveniently located and can only be accessed via the dining room, etc." This hotel no longer exists, and its erstwhile location is not known, although the sketch indicates that it faced Second Street.

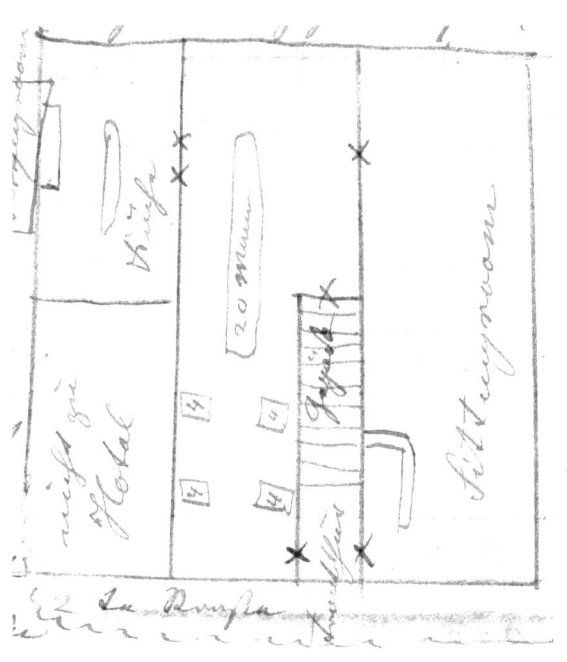

The writer included a sketch of the main floor of the Eagle Hotel, naming the rooms, clockwise from top left: kitchen, 20-person dining room, sitting room, luggage room (under stairway). "Front door" is written at bottom center, opening on 2nd Street. Writing in the bottom left corner says, "not to Hotel." X's most likely indicate doorways.
Purchase of this hotel apparently was not pursued, but the letter indicates that Claus and Johann II continued to look for commercial property in Portland.
Schlichting Letters Collection: 1882-05-18 Portland Ltr to Claus S OR

The Emigrant Letters ♦ 97

In a letter he wrote later that year on November 10, 1882, Hinrich indicated his awareness of "the Portland businesses" but wrote that there was not much he could say about them. He also wrote that he hoped Claus and Johann would "apply to your place" money he had sent, meaning paying the costs of running the farm. But he added, "maybe you'll also add more land."[146] The comment is curious, seeing that he knew about their business ventures in Portland. Was Hinrich encouraging his brothers to invest in land rather than businesses in the city? He knew that there was still much to be done to make the Middleton farm a sustainable enterprise. While encouraging them to invest in their farm or even to purchase more land, he seems generally to have trusted his brothers to make good decisions about their use of the substantial sums of money he was sending them.

Considering these actions of the brothers in Oregon—given the tenuous state of their financial affairs and the fact that they were already dependent on the infusions of cash Hinrich was sending—it seems questionable if not reckless that they would continue their costly business pursuits. Unfortunately, after this November 1882 letter from Hinrich, we have no other letter exchanges between Minnesota and Oregon through 1885.

Tragedy struck when, on June 5, 1883, Johann II died suddenly at age 39. No family correspondence or documents of any kind have yet been found that mention his death, its cause, or the circumstances around it. At that time the state of Oregon did not yet keep records of deaths; thus, searches in state records yield no information. Probate court records from 1884 reveal that he died in Portland. The only other tangible evidence remaining is the entry in the burial record of St. Paul Lutheran Church in Sherwood and the stone that marks his gravesite in the church cemetery.

Quite aside from the shock and grief that ensued for his sister and brothers and the rest of the family, probate records show that Johann's debts were substantial. His death left all financial responsibilities with Claus, who was never able to pay off the debts.

This gravestone in the St. Paul Lutheran Church cemetery in Sherwood, Oregon marks the resting place of Johann II Schlichting. The inscription reads:
"Here rests in God
JOHANN SCHLICHTING
born 26 Feb. 1844
died 5 June 1883."
Photo provided by David Schlichting

---

[146] "1882-11-10 Hinrich S MN to Claus Joh II S OR"

Before moving forward with the chronological order of correspondence in this chapter, two other letters from 1882 should be mentioned. First, on April 27, 1882, Peter Schlichting wrote to the Oregon family.[147] He began with an apology for not responding sooner to a letter they had sent. He wrote that he and his wife Maria were well but that his brother Diedrich, age 67, was ailing and had been bedridden during winter. Peter wrote that the previous summer, Anton Blank had had an opportunity to sell his little house at the Horn Mill in Neuland but did not follow through on a sale. His simple lifestyle continued much as it had. Peter wrote, "Anton fishes, keeps two sheep, and does day labor. He lives alone in his house."

In the same letter, Peter wrote about a neighbor who at age 67 wanted to emigrate to America. Peter discouraged him and wouldn't give him the address of the Oregon family. He related other news from the neighborhood, including that the village of Engelschoff wanted to build a steam-powered engine to pump water out of the polders and into the Oste River. He added that Anton B. was hoping to work on the project. He ended the letter with greetings from himself and his wife Maria, along with greetings from his sister Metta: "...to you (Claus) and Johann, and to Rebecka and her husband. We wish you well." It was signed, "Your Uncle, Peter Schlichting."

A short note from Hinrich in Minnesota, dated September 20, 1882, was directed to Johann II: "I wrote last time about the harvest. This year is as dry as last year was wet. Threshing is proceeding exceptionally, plowing not so well. We had our first frost last night. Corn is doing quite well. Prices remain unchanged. Let Claus and Rebecka read this, too."

On November 10 Hinrich wrote the letter already discussed above. In addition to those comments, he touched on a few other topics relating to the Minnesota farm:

• He noted that he had bought a binder[148] the previous year. Although several words are obscured, the name Minneapolis is legible, which probably indicates the manufacturer of the implement he bought. He wrote about prices for crops and decisions about whether to hold them a while before selling them, hoping for better prices later. And he noted yields of crops like wheat, barley, oats, corn, and potatoes, as well as livestock and products sold.

• Hinrich and a hired man had put up a great deal of fencing. He offered details: "We have fenced in 10 acres with barbed wire for $40 and 200 posts, three wires high...At that height no animal can get through."

The last two letters in this group were written by Peter Schlichting from Breitenwisch. On February 24, 1883, he wrote his nephews and niece in Oregon—Claus, Johann II, and Rebecka and her husband Thomas Matthiesen—with the news that his (and their father Johann I's) brother Diedrich had died on February 7. This left Peter and his sister Metta Hellwege the sole survivors of their generation. Metta herself had recovered from a recent illness, while Peter, his wife, and Anton Blank were all well.

He wrote that the church at Horst (the Schlichting family's ancestral parish) was laying out a new cemetery. This development is verified by the congregation's records. The "old" cemetery that had surrounded the church since its founding in the 13th century was closed in 1885. From then on, all burials took place at the new site. Today there are still several very old grave markers maintained and standing at the old cemetery site next to the church. At least two of them

---

[147] 1882-04-27 Peter S Brtnw to Claus S OR
[148] A binder—or reaper-binder—at that time was a horse-drawn farm implement that mechanically cut stalks of ripe grain in the field, pulled them together, tied them into "sheaves," and left them standing upright to dry further. Previously, this work was all done manually.

bear the Schlichting name, but the persons named were not in our family line.

Weather had been mild and crop and livestock prices favorable. Peter closed with greetings to Claus and Johann, and to Rebecka and her husband.

The next letter in this group was written by Peter almost exactly two years later, on February 17, 1885. While the end of the letter is missing, it is nonetheless filled with news:

- He began by sending greetings from himself and his wife, from Anton Blank, a Mrs. Spreckels (identity uncertain), and from his sister Metta Hellwege, sent to all the Oregon family: Claus, Rebecka and Thomas Matthiesen and their children.

- He wrote first about a man named Johann Blanck and his sisters from a community named Goetzdorf.[149] One sister, despite questionable mental competence, had legally bequeathed 12,000 Marks to "people," while Blanck himself had bequeathed his farm to a butcher in the town of Drochtersen (along the Elbe River). The estate was supposed to have been worth some 100,000 Marks. Peter indicated that Anton Blank had little to do with Johann Blanck. Whether they were related is uncertain.

- Peter reported that Uncle Anton Blank was healthy, though he expressed some concern about his overall welfare. Anton, by then 57 years old, was still working as a day laborer in the summer and in the fall did commercial fishing on the river. "He also has bees, chickens, and ducks in his new house. And he has a joyful heart."

- Neighborhood news took up the middle segment of the letter, including word that a shoemaker named Horreis was now living in the farmhouse in Neuland Oste Dike where Claus and Rebecka had grown up.

- The adult children of Peter's late brother Diedrich had not corresponded. But Peter had learned from a village elder that one son, Johann, had emigrated to America in December 1882, and that he had sent later for his wife and child.[150] Peter mentioned that Johann might seek contact with the Oregonians and asked that they notify him if that happened.

- His sister Metta Hellwege's son Johann was growing tall and was doing well in school.[151]

Peter added news about weather. The previous summer had been very warm and was followed by a cold winter. Peter's work at the locks[152] forced him to be outdoors in the weather and as a result he had become ill, though by February he had recovered. The letter is cut off mid-sentence. The remainder is missing.

---

[149] German spelling, *Götzdorf* (Peter wrote *Gätzdorf*). It is a small settlement north of Stade and about 10 miles east of Breitenwisch. Google Maps coordinates 53.63625, 9.46949.

[150] Johann and his family had settled near St. Paul, Minn. Two letters he wrote to Claus or Hinrich in Oregon in 1895 are included in the collection and will be discussed in Chapter 9. They also were reprinted in *New World Beginnings*, p. 13.

[151] Metta had been widowed since 1879 and had also lost her daughter. She lived until 1919. Her son Johann eventually married and had a family of his own. He remained in the village of Kleinwoerden, dying in 1951 at age 75. Source: church records of Hechthausen parish.

[152] The locks are located where the Horst Brook (*Horsterbeek*) empties into the Oste River near the Horst church. In a January 1875 letter, Peter had stated that he worked at the locks there. See Google Maps coordinates 53.642987, 9.278567.

Chapter 9
1886-1904
The Passing of a Generation

Date	Source	Writer in Germany / Recipient	Writer in U.S. / Recipient	Comments
1888 Mar. 22	photocopy	Peter Schlichting, Breitenwisch, to Claus S, Rebecka & Thomas Matthiesen, Ore.		News re. Anton Blank, his wife's death. Neighborhood news. Sister Metta and son well. Peter had to hire day laborers on his farm. He still worked at the Horst locks. Concern about food shortage. Crop & livestock prices. News of late brother Diedrich's children, incl. Johann in Minn. Weather cold.
1889 maybe	photocopy	Peter Schlichting, Brtnw, to probably Claus S, Rebecka M, Ore.		Incomplete and undated letter, might belong with 2/23/1889 letter. Government offices in Stade. Had received letter from Hinrich S.
1889 Feb. 23	photocopy	Peter Schlichting, Brtnw, to Claus S, Rebecka & Thomas M, Ore.		Brief note, might belong with previous letter. Sent greetings and request for news.
January 7, 1894, Peter Schlichting of Breitenwisch, Germany died, aged 61 (brother of Johann I, uncle of Hinrich, Claus, Johann II, Rebecka).					
1894 Jan. 29	photocopy	Maria Schlichting (widow of Peter), Brtnw, to Claus S, Ore., probably		Addressed to "Dear Friend." Informed of Peter's death on Jan. 7.
1894 Mar. 9	photocopy		Hinrich S, Minn. to Claus S, Ore.	Excerpt from actual letter. Informed Claus of his health status.
1894 June 14	photocopy	Metta (Schlichting) Hellwege, Kleinwoerden, to Schlichting family, Ore.		More information about her brother Peter's death and his wife Maria's suicide. Described difficult personal situation. Requested Ore. family give her their share of Peter's estate.
October 1894, Hinrich, Caroline and their children moved from Minnesota to live with Claus on the Oregon farm.					
1895 June 24	photocopy,		Johann Schlichting, Gladstone, Minn., to Hinrich or Claus S, Ore.	Acknowledged receiving letter. Introduced himself as their uncle Diedrich's son; had been in U.S. 12 years. Requested information for why they had written. In five years, he had received no news from Germany.
1895 July 20	photocopy,		Johann Schlichting, Gladstone, Minn., to Hinrich or Claus S, Ore.	Acknowledged receipt of second letter from Oregon informing him of Rebecka's death, as well as Peter and

				wife Maria's deaths. Asked about his share of inheritance. Described his location and work. Asked about his sister & brother still in Germany.
1902 Dec. 28	handwritten copy of original		Louise Hoffman, ND, to Caroline S., OR	Letter from Louise to her sister Caroline Schlichting. Ltr. copied and shared within family. Extra note added by Charlotte (Schlichting) Burnett.
1903 July 28	original		John August Schlichting (JAS), Wisconsin, to Oregon Family	He was spending summer at the Truebenbach family farm in Wisc. Wrote about people and events there and at school. Added paragraph in English to brother Henry.
1903 Dec. 22	original		JAS, IL, to parents, OR	He was spending Christmas vacation with Burger family in Dwight, Ill. Wrote about the shorthand he was learning at proseminary, along with Greek and Hebrew. Suggested Christmas gift for himself: a sewing kit and yarn for mending. Requested letters from brother Henry and Uncle Claus.
1904 Feb. 24	Copied from "Diversity Enriches..."		Henry Schlichting, OR, to JAS, IL	Lighthearted letter from Henry (16) to brother JAS (19) at school in Ill. Humorous comments on stenography JAS was learning. Wrote about matters at the Ore. farm.
1904 Mar. 4	original		JAS, WI, to parents, OR	JAS was spending time at his Wisconsin relatives' farm. Described the domestic scene. Stories about uncles Gottlieb and Christoph. Thanked for birthday greetings. He would be back in school soon.
1904 Summer (undated)	original		Caroline Schlichting, OR, to her father Michael Truebenbach, brother Christoph and his wife Eva, WI	Storm had caused casualties elsewhere in Ore. Crops doing well. Preparations for exposition in Portland. Rebecca had poison oak; Mary would visit; she & Elizabeth working, earning $50/month.

September 29, 1904, Hinrich Schlichting died in Oregon, aged 67.

1904 Oct. 23	photocopy		Henry Schlichting, OR, to John Aug. Schlichting, Ill.	Sent by Henry to his brother JAS at school in Ill. to inform him of their father Hinrich's death.
1975 Sept. 30	Copied from "Diversity Enriches..."		Rebecca Ehlers, Idaho, to daughter Evelyn Duggan	Wrote of her father Hinrich's death in 1904 and the pastor who attended him. Described her and her cousin Marie's experience, also the care of the body in the house postmortem.

During the years covered in this chapter, the exchange of letters between the American Schlichtings and their relatives in Germany was infrequent. On each continent, the people who had known each other personally were aging, and several had already died. Uncle Peter Schlichting of Breitenwisch continued writing faithfully to his nephew Claus and niece Rebecka in Oregon, and it appears that they also wrote to him. In a few letters there is indication that he also continued correspondence with Hinrich, who until October 1894 was still in Minnesota.

In a March 22, 1888, letter, Peter Schlichting wrote that Anton Blank's wife Metta had died. Information from other sources confirms that the otherwise lifelong bachelor had married. In an unpublished article, Anton Blank's relative Anton Jungclaus wrote that a fellow fisherman named Ernst Torborg introduced Anton to a widow named Metta König. They were married in May 1885. Anton was 57 years old; Metta was 43. Sadly, Metta died only a year and a half later, leaving Anton alone once again. Until his death in 1916, he maintained a simple lifestyle along the Oste River, living in the house he had built at Neuland-Horn.[153]

Other information conveyed in Peter's letter:
- A carpenter by the name of Hegener was at that time living in the house in Neuland Oste Dike where Claus and Rebecka had grown up.
- Peter's sister Metta in Kleinwoerden (Claus and Rebecka's aunt) was well. Her son Johann was 12 years old and growing tall.
- Because of his personal health limitations, Peter had had to hire day laborers to work at his farm. He was still able to work at the Horst locks, which provided at least some income to help financially. The previous fall's harvest had been good and included potatoes, and wheat for flour.
- A neighbor (and perhaps relative) Martin von Holten had sold two parcels of land he owned along the Oste River dike—the side of the dike facing the river, called the outer dike—as sources of clay to produce clay tiles. This was one way for landowners to take advantage of the heavy clay content of some of their land, which otherwise was perhaps difficult to farm, and in the case of the outer dike land was prone to flooding.
- As in the past, Peter mentioned, unhappily, that his late brother Diedrich's three adult children, including son Johann in America, didn't communicate with him. (A July 1895 letter from the same Johann implied that the siblings also did not communicate among themselves. See below.)

The letter dated February 1889 (a "23" is faintly visible on the envelope postmark) was clearly intended for Claus, and for Rebecka and Thomas Matthiesen and their children. Its primary purpose seems to have been to make contact, seeing as the only contents were a greeting and wishes for health, along with a request for news.

This February 1889 letter is the last in our collection written by Peter Schlichting. Five years later, on January 29, 1894, his wife Maria Schlichting of Breitenwisch wrote to inform Claus and the rest of the Oregon family that Peter had died earlier that month. He was 61 years old. Her letter is quoted here in full: *"With this letter, dear friend, I may not neglect to inform you respectfully that it has pleased the Lord of life and death to take my husband Peter Schlichting from this life on the 7th of this month, at the age of 61 years, after he was confined to his bed for three days. This has filled me with deepest sorrow. I remain sincerely, Maria Schlichting"*.

Peter's death was a severe blow to Maria, as another letter from June of that year would

---

[153] Information about the marriage is taken from an unpublished article by Anton Jungclaus (1871-?) titled "Thoughts from the Times of Our Forebears" (*Einige Nachrichten aus dem Leben unserer Vorfahren*), provided by Hildegard Schmoelcke and translated by Merlin Schlichting. Anton Jungclaus was Anton Blank's nephew on AB's mother's side. Statistical information source: https://ofb.genealogy.net/famreport.php?ofb=grossenwoerden&ID=I926&nachname=Blanck&modus=&lang=de

reveal. It also meant that the most faithful correspondent from the old country to the family now in America was gone. With Peter's death, only one member of that generation of our Schlichting family in Germany remained, Peter's sister Metta Hellwege.

On June 14, 1894, Metta wrote the American relatives from her home in Kleinwoerden. She reminded them that she had written earlier to inform them of her brother Peter's death. While that letter is not in our collection, in this June letter she provided details about what had happened after he died:

- After Peter's death, Metta moved to Breitenwisch to be with his widow Maria.
- Maria fell into depression. Despite Metta's personal care and medication prescribed by the doctor, on February 19 Maria took her own life by hanging.[154]
- Metta had done everything she could to help Maria, ignoring her own personal needs and those at home. She claimed that Maria's family did little to help.
- Metta was now herself emotionally drained as she wrestled with the settling of Peter's estate.
- Metta had understood from Peter that after his death, she would inherit his estate. But his marriage to Maria had complicated the matter because of a prenuptial agreement they had made. They had spent some of the money Maria had brought into the marriage—Peter had alluded to this in an 1878 letter.[155] Now after her death that amount would have to be repaid to Maria's estate.
- Once that had been paid, Peter's remaining estate would "all go to his relatives."

Metta wrote, "I turned over the house and belongings to the authorities to sell. The cow and pigs are gone because my dear brother was so weak and couldn't manage any longer. I would have liked to see his assets remain, and that I would be the sole heir in all these difficulties." But now, she explained, the estate would be divided into seven parts; that is, to all Peter's surviving nieces and nephews (Johann I's three, Diedrich's three, and Metta's own son). Metta wrote that after all requirements had been satisfied, the amount left for each person would be very small.

She then asked whether Claus and Rebecka would be willing to sign over their portion of the inheritance to her, "as a gift." Her final comment was that she was enclosing a form for them to sign, authorizing such a transfer. Unfortunately, the letter ends there in mid-sentence. Anything else she wrote or enclosed has been lost, and the question of whether Claus, Rebecka, Hinrich, or Diedrich's three adult children would agree to her request cannot be answered.

---

[154] See website, https://ofb.genealogy.net/famreport.php?ofb=burweg&ID=I13033&lang=de

[155] "1878-04-16 Peter S Brtnw to Johann I S MN."

March 9, 1894, Letter of Hinrich to Claus

A few months before Metta sent her letter, Hinrich in Minnesota had written to his brother Claus in Oregon. The letter is dated March 9. Only a short excerpt from the letter exists, and it appears in the book *Hinrich* on page 175. He wrote about his health status: "I was again somewhat ill, kind of a stomach catarrh. However, I am fairly well again, though I have been ill very frequently. Can't stand much. I did not lie in bed, but I have become very weak."[156] Hinrich's health was in fact declining, primarily because of untreated diabetes.

David Schlichting suggests in his book *Hinrich* that two primary factors drove Hinrich and Caroline to the decision to move their family to Oregon that year. First, his declining health increasingly limited his ability to farm and to support both the Minnesota and the Oregon farms.

Second, Claus in Oregon was in dire financial straits due to debts he could not repay.[157] John August Schlichting also held the opinion that his father's declining health was one reason for the move, though he did not mention the serious financial issues with the Oregon farm.[158]

Hinrich and Caroline moved their family to Oregon in October of 1894, but they did not sell any of their Minnesota property. Caroline, then 41, was pregnant with their seventh child. Their son John August, just nine years old at the time of the long train journey west, wrote a surprisingly comprehensive account of the trip in his memoir.[159] On January 18, 1895, while they were still settling into their new home and responsibilities on the Oregon farm, Hinrich and Caroline welcomed their newest addition, daughter Rebecca.

The Hinrich and Caroline Schlichting family, photographed in 1891 while the family was living on their farm near Lake City, Minnesota. The photo frame named the Wood studio in Lake City.

The children and their ages in 1891 were daughters Mary (9), Elizabeth (10), and sons John August (6), Ernst (1) on Caroline's lap, and Henry (4). Another daughter, Caroline, had died shortly after her birth in 1886.

The family moved west to Oregon in October 1894, while Caroline was pregnant with their youngest child, Rebecca, who was born in January 1895. Schlichting family photo collection.

---

[156] The excerpt is from a longer letter that is no longer extant. The excerpt is available only in a translation made by John August Schlichting and was drawn from the Dorothy Schlichting collection in Oregon.

[157] *Hinrich*, pp. 175-176.
[158] *As I Remember*, p. 25.
[159] Op. cit. pp. 12-13.

Less than three months later, on March 2, 1895, Hinrich's sister Rebecka Matthiesen died of pneumonia at age 41, leaving behind her husband Thomas and their eight children, including the youngest, Marie, who was just eight months old. Realizing that he could not manage to care for an infant and his older children while farming full time, Thomas entrusted Marie to the care of Caroline and Hinrich. The farms of the two families were not far apart, and Hinrich and Caroline made sure that Marie had frequent contact with her birth family. In the Schlichting family, although she was a cousin, Marie grew up as a sister to the Schlichting children. She was especially close to her almost same-aged cousin Rebecca. The two girls ended up marrying brothers, Edwin and Emil Ehlers, and lived on farms near Twin Falls, Idaho.

1895 Letters of Johann Schlichting, Saint Paul (Gladstone), Minn., to Claus or Hinrich Schlichting, Oregon

Sometime during the first part of 1895, either Hinrich or Claus tried to contact their cousin Johann Schlichting in Minnesota. Johann was a son of their father's brother Diedrich.[160] (In his March 2, 1888, letter—see above—Peter had written that Johann was in America.) Claus and Hinrich's purpose in writing was to clarify whether this Johann was indeed their cousin before they sent personal news regarding Rebecka's death, and the deaths of Peter and Maria Schlichting in Germany the previous year. How they knew to write Johann in Minnesota is not clear, but Johann had lived there since 1883, and Hinrich, who at that time was farming near Lake City, might have become aware of it. The letters Hinrich or Claus sent from Oregon to Johann in Minnesota have been lost. But two responses Johann wrote from Gladstone have been preserved and are included in the letters collection.[161]

Gladstone, the village where Johann was living, was only three miles from St. Paul; today it is part of the St. Paul suburb of Maplewood. It seems that Claus or Hinrich had written to Johann to establish contact. They had been cautious about how much information they sent until they were certain that he was indeed the cousin they were seeking. In his first response on June 24, Johann exhibited an equally cautious approach, writing in the formal style of a business letter: "Dear Mr. Schlichting." He also used the formal personal pronoun *Sie*. Had he known with certainty that he was writing to his cousin, Johann would have addressed his letter to the writer by first name and used the informal personal pronoun *Du*.

As confirmation of his identity, Johann wrote in his June 24 letter, "I have been in America for 12 years. I am Diederich Schlichting's son from Breitenwisch, in the district of Stade and jurisdiction of Himmelpforten. If I am the person you are seeking, I would like to know with whom I have the honor [of corresponding] and what it is about." Johann added that in five-and-a-half years, he had heard nothing from his brother and sister in Germany, despite having written to them. He closed by asking for a response.

With Johann's identity confirmed, either Hinrich or Claus wrote again—this letter also is not in our collection—informing him both of their sister Rebecka's death on March 5 and of the deaths of Peter and Maria in Germany in early 1894. On July 20, Johann sent his reply: "Dear Cousins, I received your letter and was very happy to have heard from you ... I am very sorry

---

[160] His name was also spelled Diederich.

[161] They also were translated and included in *New World Beginnings for the Schlichting Family*, on page 13.

that Rebecka has died already. You also wrote that Uncle Peter and his wife have died. I am very sorry about that. When did they die? Please be so good and write what my portion [of the inheritance] amounts to."[162]

Johann went on to explain that he had bought three acres of land in Gladstone for $600 and that he made his living growing garden produce. He had two horses and a cow. He also asked for information about his brother and sister in Germany. What Johann did not write was that he was living in Gladstone with his family. According to the 1900 census report, the family consisted of Johann, his wife Minnie, and two daughters, Anna and Minnie.

1900 census data showed Johann ("John") Schlichting, his wife Minnie, and daughters Anna (20) and Minnie (13), living in New Canada Township, Ramsey County, Minnesota. Daughter Anna had been born in Germany; Minnie was born in Minnesota. Johann's profession was given as "Gardener," consistent with what he wrote in his July 20, 1895, letter to Hinrich and Claus.

Source: Ancestry.com. 1900 United States Federal Census [database on-line], Provo, UT, USA: Ancestry.com Operations Inc, 2004

As was the case with the Oregon Schlichting family, there is no word about whether Johann eventually received his share of Peter's estate, or whether he was informed of his Aunt Metta's request to sign over his share to her.

December 28, 1902, Letter of Louise Hoffman, North Dakota, to Caroline Schlichting, Oregon

This letter falls outside the usual parameters of our collection, but its story is interesting. It was found in a box containing various letters and articles saved with John August Schlichting's papers. The letter's writer was Louise Hoffman, who was farming with her husband Fritz near Grand Rapids, North Dakota. Louise Hoffman and Caroline Schlichting were Truebenbach sisters. The long, newsy letter Louise sent to her sister is filled with information about their family, Louise's neighborhood, and acquaintances known to both sisters.

Written in German, the letter followed a circuitous route. It was sent first to Caroline in Oregon, then it was passed from one to another of her teenage or young adult children. Finally, it was copied verbatim and sent to 17-year-old son John August—he had started proseminary in Springfield, Illinois that fall—by his older sister Mary. It is this copy that has been preserved. Mary transcribed it in the *Kurrent* German style of handwriting (no doubt the same as Louise's original). From a comment Mary wrote in English on an extra page, the transcribing must have been an arduous task: "John, if I knew before I

---

[162] Johann began this letter with the greeting "Dear Cousins." In the body of the letter, he used both singular and plural personal pronouns, which indicates that he was writing to both Hinrich and Claus.

started that Aunt Louise [sic] letter was so long, I should never have tried to copy it, but every word seemed too interesting to leave out ... I hope you will enjoy it to read ... [Louise] sent the letter home (the Oregon farm). Henry (then 15) sent it to Lizzie (sister Elizabeth, 21), she gave it to me. I copied it for you ... Remain as ever, Your loving sister"

While this letter is only tangentially related to most of the letters in the collection, it is a reminder of at least two things:

First, at that time letter-writing was crucially important for maintaining contact with people. Regardless of the distance between them, people wrote letters, many letters. We may assume that what we have in our collection today is but a small portion of the total number of letters sent and received. Yet, even if our collection represents just a part of the total output, it is clear that what was shared in the letters was important for both writer and recipient, as a source of information, and as a means of staying close to those who mattered most.

Second, nearly all the letters in our collection, including those written by younger people, were written in German, in the *Kurrent* style of handwriting that was commonly used then. Despite the challenge both the language and the handwriting present to readers today, it shows that these young people, members of the first American-born generation, were bilingual. They still understood, spoke, and could write their parents' German, while they also learned English. Except for John August, none of them received more than a sixth or perhaps eighth grade education, and yet they were able to communicate in both the old language and the new. This pattern of acculturation has been common to every immigrant group that has come to the United States, including our own forebears.

John August and Seminary

It has already been noted that John August Schlichting, Hinrich and Caroline's oldest son, had decided to seek ordained ministry in the Lutheran church. This presented a two-part challenge. First, becoming a pastor required candidates to enroll in and graduate from the church's seminary. Although John August had received an elementary school education—at a public school in Minnesota, then the parochial school of the Lutheran congregation in Sherwood and limited time at a public school there—he had no opportunity to attend high school.

The Lutheran Church-Missouri Synod, the church body of which the Sherwood congregation was a part, offered a kind of work-around for potential students who, like John August, had no opportunity to attend college (or in his case even high school). At their seminary in Springfield, Illinois, the church had started what it called a pro-seminary. It was a kind of preparatory school for seminary. Students typically enrolled for a two-year course of study, where among other subjects they began studies in Latin and biblical Greek. The LC-MS had strong German roots. The faculty was proficient in German, and classes were taught in that language. This made it easier for German-speaking students to tackle those other languages and subjects. It was this approach John August would take.

In Chapter 4, two letters were discussed which reveal that John August's father Hinrich had himself, at the end of 1874, made inquiries at the Springfield school. At the time he was 38 years old, unmarried, and was farming near Lake City, Minnesota. He did not follow through on the recommendations sent to him by a Professor Craemer, who wrote from St. Louis, Missouri. But now his oldest son desired to follow the same course. This presented Hinrich with a dilemma, the second part of the challenge.

Some background will help to explain. While the family lived in Minnesota, Hinrich had a positive relationship with the pastors and fellow members of the Lutheran congregation in Jacksonville. It too was part of the Missouri Synod, and Hinrich had played a vital role in the congregation's founding—he literally built much of the church, including the altar and pulpit. After he and Caroline Truebenbach married in mid-1880 (the first wedding in the congregation's parish record), and as their children were born and reached school age, they attended the one-room public school in Jacksonville. The three oldest, Elizabeth, Mary, and John August, all finished several years of school. But by the time their second son, Henry, came of school age in fall, 1894, Hinrich and Caroline were about to move their family to Oregon. Thus, Henry probably—and his younger brother Ernst certainly—did not even begin school until the family was living on the farm in Sherwood, Oregon.

After arriving in Sherwood in October 1894—as Middleton had been renamed—Hinrich quickly sought membership in the St. Paul Lutheran congregation there. Unfortunately, the relationship with the pastor then serving at the church, who also was the teacher in the small congregation's parochial school—the "German school"—was nowhere near as cordial as in Jacksonville.[163] John August wrote later in his memoir that the pastor proved to be contentious and argumentative, and that he employed martial means of discipline in the school. Corporal punishment was common and included beatings and whippings of both boys and girls with a shortened buggy whip, often for minor infractions. Among those so punished was John August's younger brother Henry. John August wrote, "...when [Henry] was so horribly beaten my heart went out to him in deep sympathy, and I began to hate all that was in connection with the school. Some red welts showed up where the 'black stick' had struck. That filled me with more rebellion than ever against the school..." He resolved that should he ever receive such abuse he would run away. "I too knew where to buy a ticket ... in Portland."[164] He never forgot the abuse at that school, as a letter he wrote near the end of his life would testify. It will be discussed in the next chapter.

John August learned that his father Hinrich "...had seen the minister and remonstrated with him over his whipping the children so terribly. I told Father we had no arithmetic, no geography, no grammar, no English reading such as we had in Minnesota."[165] He wrote that the situation improved somewhat, but a sour taste remained, both with John August and with his father.

This is what presented Hinrich with a dilemma when, sometime after John August had been confirmed in 1899, he asked his father's permission to attend "college" (the proseminary) and to seek ordination to the ministry. In *As I Remember*, John August recalled both the strong call to ministry he sensed and anxiety that the beatings meted out at the parochial school in Sherwood would continue in college. His mother wasn't so sure about that, but when the teenager asked about pursuing studies toward the ministry, his father pronounced a resounding "No!" Given recent experience, Hinrich's reaction was understandable: "[Father] said the pastors were too self-opinionated and quarrelsome" (*zu rechthaberisch und streitsuechtig*).[166]

In time, however, Hinrich relented and gave his consent. The young man entered the proseminary in Springfield, Illinois, in the fall of 1902 when he was 17 years old. John August later

---

[163] The pastor was Carl J.M. Heuer, who served the congregation 1892-1898.
[164] *As I Remember*, p. 22-23.
[165] Op. cit., p. 22.
[166] Op. cit., p. 29.

wrote how much he treasured the letters his father wrote him while he was at school, and the wise advice they contained.

At that time, John August was unaware that his father had himself once inquired about study at the Springfield proseminary and seminary. Years later, his brother Ernst made him aware of the letters Professor Craemer had sent to Hinrich in late 1874 and early 1875 (see Chapter 4). In *New World Beginnings for the Schlichting Family*, a comment by John August was reprinted: "Brother Ernst was right. It was our father who applied for entry into the ministry of our Synod. Note the date—ca. December, 1874 ... The love of Christ was deeply embedded in his heart—so with the rest of the family. I thank my God for the fine faith found in the hearts and minds of my forefathers."[167]

John August wrote at length in *As I Remember* about his time at the Illinois school. Of particular interest for this book, however, are three letters in our collection that he wrote to his parents and family in Oregon in 1903 and 1904, the two years he was a student at the proseminary.

July 28, 1903, Letter of John August, in Wisconsin, to his parents and siblings, Oregon

This letter of John August was written in German in the *Kurrent* handwriting style and was addressed to his parents, sisters, and brothers (*Liebe Eltern und Geschwister*). John August was spending summer vacation with his mother's Truebenbach family in Wisconsin. It was the first time he had met his maternal grandfather, Michael Truebenbach.[168] Now 18, he wrote about what he did to help on the farm. He also noted how pleased his grandfather was to have received a letter from his daughter Caroline in Oregon. "He still can read almost every letter without glasses," John August wrote. "He says, 'Best greetings always from your old father.'"

It seems younger brother Henry (15) had teased in a letter—not in our collection—that his brother was taking life easy on the farm. John countered by describing what he was doing: "I work the entire time, from early morning till late evening. Right now there's a thunderstorm, but I just returned from setting up the barley (setting the ripened and cut grain upright into sheaves in preparation for threshing). And this morning we mowed the seed clover."

He did not forget his younger siblings, calling out Marie who had celebrated her birthday on July 23: "I was thinking about Marie when she turned nine years old—already when she got up that morning. For a nine-year-old, Marie writes very well. The two of you (Marie & his youngest sister Rebecca) were very energetic about picking [berries]."[169]

In this letter, John August paid special attention to his 15-year-old brother Henry, encouraging him to continue with school, and perhaps even to join him at the proseminary in Illinois: "For Henry: I got good grades, and you can use that as your guide. You just have to want it and have the motivation for it. Just don't be afraid and back away from it. It will be all right; you are in God's hand. You can turn your disadvantages into advantages. But you have to decide soon."

His older brother knew the difficult years Henry had spent in the "German school" in Sherwood and the abuse he had suffered at the hand

---

[167] *New World Beginnings for the Schlichting Family*, p. 10. The source of John August's comment was not provided.
[168] *As I Remember*, p. 31.

[169] As discussed above, Marie was taken into Hinrich and Caroline's family after her mother, Rebecka (Schlichting) Matthiesen died of pneumonia in March 1895. Though she was a first cousin, the Schlichting children considered her their sister.

of the pastor. In this letter he encouraged Henry not to let those "disadvantages," as he called them, cause him to give up on education but to join John August at proseminary (he called it "college"). There they could be together and learn together. And there was more.

John August wrote a final paragraph in English and directed it to Henry: "[I] would like to see you join this fall. Do according to your saying, and you will never regret. Also I can assure you that next year you will be tired of farming, and not knowing what to do...I would rather return to College now if I could. Reason: Get better grub there than here. Besides in College you don't always have to study, sometimes you will fool around more than you have to. Write a slip of paper next time about it. I can keep it secret. Your opinion. Don't bring that worn out excuse that the farm will go to destruction."

That John August wrote that final paragraph in English, while the rest of the letter was German, indicates that he really wanted Henry to read it, and probably hoped their parents would not bother with it. While by that time both Hinrich and Caroline certainly could read English, it was still a foreign language to them, and it would have taken effort to read it. This was a message aimed specifically at Henry. But what John August was asking was problematic.

He was asking that Henry leave the farm and, like him, pursue an education. That might have been an admirable thought, but what he did not take into consideration in his youthful enthusiasm was how that would affect their parents and the farm itself. One son had already left to pursue an education. What would happen if a second son left? Henry's departure would have left youngest brother Ernst (then just 13), his father Hinrich (who was not well), and their Uncle Claus (by then 63) to tend to a 265-acre farm.

As it turned out, Henry had no interest in further education. His love was farming. As the years in Oregon went by, he and his brother Ernst would increasingly take on the bulk of the farm work. Their father's untreated diabetic condition left him weakened, but under his guidance and with the strong support of their mother and whatever help their Uncle Claus could give, the boys were turning the Oregon farm into a thriving enterprise.

Later letters in our collection between John August and Henry show that while they would remain close, their lives would follow different trajectories.

December 22, 1903, Letter of John August, Illinois, to his parents in Oregon

John August wrote this letter, in German, to his parents while spending the Christmas holiday with a family named Burger in Dwight, Illinois. In the letter, he responded to topics that obviously had been raised in letters he had received from home. The letter also reveals the new, broader world he, at age 18, was being introduced to as his education at proseminary proceeded.

In the first months of his second year at school he had been introduced to New Testament Greek, and to Hebrew. Already fluent in both German and English, he now was adding a third and a fourth language. In a jesting boast, he wrote, "We are also learning Greek and Hebrew. In a pinch I could deceive someone in Greek—I've learned most of the letters [of the Greek alphabet]."

He also was learning to use a tool that would help him in his studies and for the rest of his life—shorthand. Exactly what this shorthand was is not described, except that an Australian classmate had introduced him to it.[170] He continued, "You can learn everything about shorthand from a booklet that costs 15 cents. I could have made this letter half as long, but I thought I should write well and carefully. Maybe Papa could try it and then have me read it."[171]

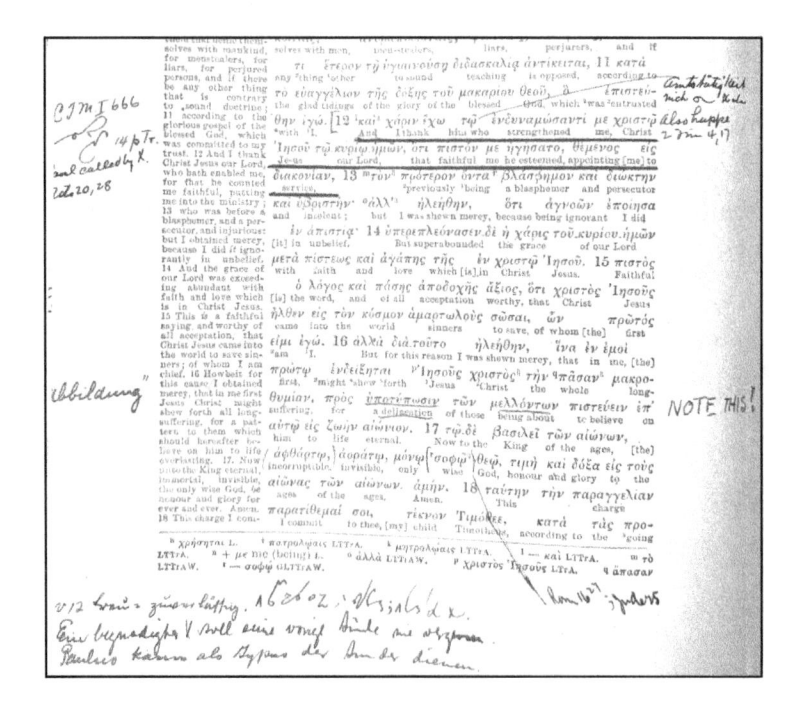

A photo of a page from John August's interlinear Greek-English New Testament displays his notes: in English, in German, and in the shorthand he learned during proseminary studies. The excerpt is from the First Letter to Timothy, Chapter 1.

---

[170] *As I Remember*, p. 30.

[171] John August's Greek-English interlinear New Testament was given to me by his widow Emma, shortly before I entered seminary in 1968. In many of the page margins he had written brief notes or reminders, as the illustration shows. I still use the book occasionally as a resource, and those added notes always recall him to mind. —MS

Merlin Schlichting ♦ 112

After confessing to being too "stingy" (he wrote the English word), John August suggested a Christmas gift: "...as far as I'm concerned, you could give me a sewing outfit as a gift. I have used up all the yarn and had to buy more." He meant it as a humorous comment, but it is also a reminder that the money his education cost was an extra burden for his parents, and he was aware of it. He ended the letter by asking Henry to write "whether the foals are as big as The Brown," and then added a postscript: "I would love to get another letter from Uncle [Claus]."

February 24, 1904, Letter of Henry Schlichting, Oregon, to his brother John August, Illinois

The next letter in the sequence was written by Henry. He had turned 16 in December 1903. The letter was printed, in English, in the booklet *Diversity Enriches the Family History*.[172] The original letter is no longer present, and the source of this copy is not indicated. Whether he wrote in German or English is hard to determine. But judging from the many inserted question marks, the person who transcribed (or translated) it obviously had difficulty deciphering Henry's writing. The letter is lighthearted in tone and filled with ironic and even ludicrous comments.

Some six months earlier in his July 28, 1903, letter, John August had asked for a response from Henry about possibly joining John at college (the part of the letter he wrote in English): "Write a slip of paper next time about it. I can keep it secret." Might this February letter have been Henry's "slip of paper" response? It is certainly possible. After making an awkward and comical reference to Latin, he wrote, "That is all the whishit, old Nudelmudel, that is all. You must have better eating than we have. I can't find no head or tail to stenography (a reference to John's shorthand). Well... you will show me how to grab the tail, when you come home..."

He then continued with farm news: "...for the last month I have been hauling potatoes two sacks to the load...we do quite a bit with the colts haul wood, go to Matthiesen (his cousins), haul wheat around the neighborhood...I know that you want to hear something from the farm, and that is all right too. I got enough of driving wagon and all such stuff pretty hard. I rather sit down and read something about the war and I like to study English Catechism." Which war he meant is unclear, but he apparently liked reading and was content to study the catechism, in English, not German.

March 4, 1904, Letter of John August, Fredonia, Wisconsin, to his parents in Oregon

Just a few weeks later, John August wrote from his Fredonia, Wisconsin, relatives' farm. He was now in his second year of study at the proseminary and should have been at school in Springfield, Ill. But an outbreak of smallpox had closed the school temporarily and the students had been sent away.[173] John August and a classmate named Herman Atrops—a fellow Oregonian who later became a relative by marriage—spent the time at the Wisconsin farm.

In his letter he wrote in the moment about the Wisconsin family as they sat in the warm room: "Hermann [Atrops] and Paul [174] are sitting with me at a 5x5 table. Hermann wants to take a bite into Latin—but who wants to eat soap? Paul wants to write. Uncle Christoph is eagerly

---

[172] Op. cit., p. 45.
[173] *As I Remember*, p. 31.

[174] "Hermann" was no doubt Herman Atrops (here JAS spelled his first name in the German manner). Paul's identity is uncertain.

studying the newspaper, while Aunt Eva is sitting behind the stove, maintaining that it's very nice there ... Outside, grim. Jack Frost grips you with his iron-like claws. Not good weather for snowballs, but you can walk on top of the snow." It was a description of a serious cold snap in early March. His parents doubtless would remember such weather from their many years in Minnesota. John August ended on a lighthearted note: "Don't be at all concerned about me; mostly I get by as free as a bird. Back to college soon, a few tests, then I'm free—hurrah. Thanks for the birthday greetings (he had turned 19 on February 27) ... How much are Johnny and Peter getting? (his Matthiesen cousins). If you see them, ask if they have forgotten me. They ought to write."

In the spring of 1904 John August completed his proseminary studies. In fall he would begin seminary proper. During the summer, he was able to travel back home to Oregon for the first time since the fall of 1902. He described his homecoming in *As I Remember*: "Since I could not inform the home folks of my arrival at Sherwood by train, it was up to me to walk home. We had no telephone those days. On the way home I met Rev. Spleiss (then the pastor at St. Paul Lutheran Church) and he asked me several times whether I had passed [my classes]. Father was at the picket fence gate. I saw that he had grown perceptibly older. I passed by him rather perfunctorily lest I would have to break down and cry. And mother and the rest were there too."[175]

Hinrich Schlichting was in the last months of his life. Diabetes was a condition for which there was no cure, and at that time there were few ways to control it. He had been dealing with it for many years; indeed, it was one of the reasons he and Caroline had decided to leave their successful Minnesota farm and relocate to Oregon, where Hinrich's brother Claus and sister Rebecka lived. That John August would describe his appearance as "perceptibly older" indicates the advance of his father's condition.[176]

John August described that summer's outside work in *As I Remember*. He recalled that all the men in the family worked to clear trees and stumps to create more arable land. This included Hinrich, Uncle Claus, John August, Henry, and Ernst. It is possible that hired men were enlisted as well. John August's description is brief but engrossing, and it is a reminder that preparing land for crops on the Oregon farm took place over many years and involved intense labor: "The logs on the [forty-acre plot]...were rolled into piles. There was Brownie the race horse, [P]ony the little buckskin, and Blackie. Getting the tripple-trees [sic] and the poles lined up so the logs could be rolled up, was a real job..."

---

[175] Op. cit., p. 32.

[176] Ibid.

John August wrote about clearing logs from land on the Oregon farm in the summer of 1904, using "triple-trees," a combination of harnesses and chains to skid logs. The devices are called "eveners." They are attached to the rear harness gear of a span of horses, then by chain and cross-spars to the logs. This photo shows a double-tree evener, made for two horses. In Oregon, the Schlichtings had their three horses Brownie, Pony, and Blackie to pull the logs, so they used a triple-tree evener. John August described the challenge of skidding logs with this complicated setup and moving them onto a pile. He added, "Then came the day of burning and what a burning it was! How different the place began to look!" As I Remember, p. 32. Photo courtesy of the Minnesota Forest History Center, John Beltman, Program Supervisor

It was stated above that when John August arrived home for the summer, he saw how much his father had aged, due in large measure to the diabetes with which Hinrich had been dealing for so many years. But despite growing weakness, Hinrich toiled alongside his sons and brother through the summer. In later retrospection, John August wrote of the toll it took on his father: "Father worked hard at it (so did we all), and several times all father's clothes were wet, wet with sweat as though he had fallen into some vat. This was not a wholesome sweat."[177]

The Schlichting family at the Oregon farm in summer 1902, or possibly 1904. From left: Elizabeth, Mary, Henry, Ernst, John August, Uncle Claus. Girls in front: Marie (Matthiesen) and Rebecca. Sitting: Caroline and Hinrich.

Photo from the Schlichting family collection

---

[177] Op. cit., p. 32.

The Emigrant Letters • 115

Summer 1904 Letter of Caroline Schlichting, Oregon, to her family in Wisconsin

This undated letter of Caroline Schlichting was written at the Oregon farm in 1904, in mid to late summer. Caroline wrote it to her father Michael Truebenbach, and her brother Christoph and his wife Eva at their farm near Fredonia, Wisconsin. This was the family John August had stayed with during the summer of 1903 and then in March of 1904.

Caroline began by writing about a severe storm elsewhere in Oregon that had taken several lives, and that aid for relief had been sent from Portland. She wrote that the farm crops and work were proceeding. Haymaking was going well, the winter wheat was ripening, and the fruit trees were all bearing. Prices for cattle and fowl were good, also for butter and other products. She also wrote about "...work being done where the exposition is to take place." This was a reference to construction and building for the Lewis and Clark Centennial Exposition that would take place in Portland in summer and fall 1905.

Caroline also wrote about her children. Rebecca (age 9) had a bad case of poison oak on her face and hands. Son John August (she wrote "Johan") had identified it, and fortunately it was improving. Daughter Mary (21 that summer) would be home for two weeks—a welcome visit—while daughter Elizabeth (23 – Caroline wrote "Lizzie") had visited at Pentecost (May 22 that year), along with a Mrs. Burell. Both her older daughters were working in domestic settings in Portland and, she wrote, were earning $50 per month.

Determining a time for the letter's writing is based primarily on her note about the exposition, and that son John August was home for the summer. It was the first time he'd been back since leaving for proseminary in Springfield, Illinois in late summer 1902. He had now finished his two years of study at the proseminary. Late that summer he returned to Springfield to commence studies at Concordia Seminary.

On September 12, Hinrich turned 67, but his health was deteriorating quickly. He died on September 29. At school in Illinois, John August received a telegram from his sister Elizabeth consisting of three words: "Father is dead." At first, he thought "some mishap" had befallen his father. But a few days later a letter arrived—not in our collection—stating that his father's condition was getting worse. He knew then that there had been no accident.[178]

It is a letter that younger brother Henry sent to John August, dated October 23, 1904, that describes the course of their father's final days and hours. It is truly a gift to have that letter preserved, and in English. It was printed in *New World Beginnings for the Schlichting Family* on page 12, along with an introduction by John August. It is copied here in its entirety. Whether Henry wrote in German or English is not certain, but from the wording and especially the ending it seems likely that this is an edited version:

---

[178] Ibid.

Sherwood, Oregon
October 23, 1904
Dear John,

We received your last letter some time ago and I sent the order of $20.00 yesterday. Now it is three weeks that our father is home. We know it was God's will. This shall be done. I will try to give you the story of his sickness, death, and burial as nearly as I can. His sickness was diabetes, or sugar in the urine. This sickness, as the doctor says, had been working in him for years and now it broke out, and so at once heart and lungs were weakened after being in bed one day. He was not very sick. One morning about three o'clock he became suddenly short of breath, so that with his mouth wide open he had great difficulty getting air. This spell lasted two hours. Then for two, three days it kept on. No appetite, he would only drink a little soup, and he asked that we rub him on the face and hands, legs, and breast.

On Saturday evening he was at times nearly gone, out of breath, I mean. Pastor Doering then gave him the Lord's Supper. He could scarcely breathe but just pressed the sound out, in German, "O Christ, Thou Lamb of God." It was about midnight when he gave Doering his hand and said he hoped for a reunion in heaven.

Thomas Matthiesen (Hinrich's brother-in-law) was always with us. Father nearly always had his hands folded and was never out of his senses. Three or four days passed like that.

He spoke much about you and K. (Hinrich's son-in-law Henry Koppelmann) and all friends. He asked especially to send you and K. a telegram if he should die and said his funeral text should be "Weep not for me," etc. (a reference to Luke 8:52 or possibly 23:28).

He said so much that I could not write it all in days. I will write more of this and answer your questions, if you wish to know more.

Wednesday night the spell came again. Throughout the day he would say, "Oh now it is soon coming again. But I am so weak. Jesus will help soon, for I am going home." Always something about God.

About ten o'clock he said in German, "I want to count you all again in heaven: Mama, Elizabeth, Mary, Johann, Henry, Ernst, Becka, Uncle Thomas and all his children, and many others I will see in heaven. Live in peace with one another, for I am going home."

He said much more that could not be understood. He always prayed until he no longer could fold his hands, for they were already getting cold. He had held the Bible in his hands and said we should treasure the books from which we had read him so many passages. His death struggle lasted from three until five o'clock, and then he fell asleep in the Lord to enter the heavenly harbor to be with God."

Henry then closes with the following prayer: "God grant that our end may be a blessed one and that we may die with firm confidence in the Lord. God grant it."

Then a sort of postscript: I'll write more another time. May this be our word of comfort: Weep not, etc.

My father: Henry Schlichting
*   Born September 12, 1837*
*   Died September 29, 1904*
*   Age, 67 years.*

September 30, 1975, Letter of Rebecca (Schlichting) Ehlers, Idaho, to her daughter Evelyn Duggan

Another letter, written decades later by Hinrich and Caroline's youngest daughter Rebecca to her daughter Evelyn Duggan, also described the event of Hinrich's passing. Rebecca wrote it when she was 80 years old (she lived to the age of 89, dying in 1984). At the time of her father's death, she was only nine years old, but her memory of it was clear: "...[the pastor] came one night and we all gathered round [father's] bed (he had a hard time getting his breath) and all except Marie and I took Communion. We were 9-10 years old at the time. Two nights later he died, they didn't waken Marie and I [sic] that night, but sister Mary came to our bed in the morning and said father had gone to heaven."[179]

In her letter, Rebecca added a comment that reminds us of Hinrich's physical stature. She wrote that after he died, "the corpse was kept in the home ... and a number of days passed before a long enough coffin could be sent out from Portland. Tubs of cold water were kept in the room."[180] According to his 1865 military discharge papers, Hinrich was six feet, three and-a-half inches tall. He had served in the Hanoverian Regimental Guard (*Garde-Regiment Hannover*).[181] Requirements for serving in the guard were that a man had to be at least 6' 1" tall, without shoes. His younger brother Johann II also served in that regiment.

The death of Hinrich Schlichting on September 29, 1904, marked the end of a memorable life. In his book *Hinrich*, David Schlichting wrote, "It would be difficult to overstate the central role Hinrich Schlichting played in his family. His success at raising his own family was equaled only by the support he provided for his siblings and father. At every turn of events, he was the leader of the immigrant family. From Germany to Cincinnati, Milwaukee, Minnesota and Oregon it was Hinrich who either directly led the family or provided financial support to his siblings who were unable to meet their obligations. He left almost no written documents from his life, but his accomplishments speak for him. He was unafraid of taking risks, and somehow he was able to convert his missteps into success. The soul of his character was a quiet self-confidence. He was a leader without needing to announce it. The first American generation, his children, owed their opportunities in the 20th century to this quiet and capable man."[182]

---

[179] *Diversity Enriches the Family History...*, p. 132.
[180] Ibid.
[181] *Hinrich*, p. 19.
[182] Op. cit., pp. 195-196.

CHAPTER 10

1905 AND BEYOND

The Next Generation and the Tie that Binds

Date	Source	Writer in Germany / Recipient	Writer in U.S. / Recipient	Comments
1906 Apr. 31 (*sic*)	*Diversity Enriches the Family...*		Ernst S, Portland, Ore., to Henry S, Ore. farm	Written while Ernst was at Concordia School and perhaps living with sister Elizabeth.
1909 Oct. 9	photocopy		Henry S, Minn., to Claus S, Ore.	"Land deal" in Minn. Henry was tending the Minn. farm but planned to return to Ore. Parents were well remembered. Personal matter re. Claus.
1911 Mar. 9	Doris Mundhenk, from JA Schlichting papers		Caroline Schlichting, Ore., to JA Schlichting, Wash.	Caroline wrote to her son at his first parish in Wash. Sent information about his siblings and their families.
1913 Aug. 17	*NewWorld Beginnings* p. 16		Caroline Schlichting, Ore., to Rebecca S, Ore.	Wrote to acknowledge Rebecca's engagement to Edwin Ehlers.
1913 Aug. 29	*New World Beginnings* p. 17		Caroline Schlichting, Ore., to Edwin Ehlers, Idaho	Wrote to give her blessing to Edwin's marriage to Rebecca.
December 10, 1913, Rebecca Schlichting and Edwin Ehlers married, began farming near Twin Falls, Idaho.				
1914	Photocopy	Anton Jungclaus, Neuland to Claus S, Ore.		Written on behalf of Anton Blank to inform that AB was growing weaker. Neighborhood news.
1914 May 28	Scan of original letter		JA Schlichting, Idaho, to Claus S, Ore.	Typed in German from his parish in Idaho. Asked about "the uncle" in Germany. Rebecca Ehlers was ill. His sister Elizabeth in Portland also was ill. Sausage & ham had arrived.
June 23, 1915, Marie Matthiesen and Emil Ehlers married, began farming near Twin Falls, Idaho.				
July 2, 1915, Claus Schlichting died in Oregon, aged 75.				
November 13, 1915, Elizabeth (Schlichting) Koppelmann died in Oregon of tuberculosis, aged 34.				
March 3, 1916, Anton Blank died in Neuland, Germany, aged 87 (uncle of Hinrich, Claus, Johann II, and Rebecka).				
1916 Aug. 20	*Diversity Enriches the Family...*		Henry S, Minn., to Oregon family.	Had received letter from Ernst. Good crop yield, good prices; threshing nearly finished. "Land boom" had cooled off. Greetings to Marie M.

The Emigrant Letters ♦ 119

1919 Nov. 10	Scan of original letter		Henry S, Minn., to JA Schlichting, Idaho	Written on township letterhead. Update on harvest. Described progress of farm sale and purchase. News of Fred Schumann's death; visit from Ernst Truebenbach. Relayed a one-liner from Knopp, an acquaintance.
1965 May 15	Copy of original, from the papers of JAS		JA Schlichting, Calif., to Ernst S, Ore., Rebecca Ehlers, Idaho, & their spouses	Typed letter recalling at length his confirmation day in 1899. Remembering about their father and mother.

In Chapter 4 a comment was made about the importance of letter-writing for people during the time covered in this book. It was the primary means of maintaining contact with people, whether they lived nearby or far away. This was as true for our Schlichting family as for any others. In this chapter, there will be discussion of several letters that were written after Hinrich Schlichting's death in 1904. The letters come from several sources and were written by various members of the family. As each letter is dealt with, its source will be identified as well as possible. Other letters are still available in reference sources, but these have been selected for inclusion to help illustrate how the family navigated forward in the years following Hinrich's passing.

In the first family histories—*New World Beginnings for the Schlichting Family* (1989), and *Diversity Enriches the Family History: The Schlichting Story 1914-1990* (1990)—numerous letters or parts of letters and photos were reprinted, with comments added by Hinrich and Caroline's grandchildren. Family tree charts in those booklets help the reader identify each writer's place in the several families involved. The situation of the family after Hinrich's death in late September 1904 was as follows:[183]

- Hinrich's widow Caroline (51) was living on the Oregon family farm, together with Uncle Claus (64).
- Sons Henry (nearly 17) and Ernst (14), daughter Rebecca (9) and niece Marie Matthiesen (10) also were living on the farm.
- Oldest daughter Elizabeth (23) was engaged to be married to Pastor Hermann Koppelmann. They were married on Nov. 17 at home on the farm. They would live in Portland.
- Second daughter Mary (21) was working as a domestic helper in Portland.
- Son John August (19) had returned to Springfield, Illinois, in late August or early September to study at the seminary.

Teenage sons Henry and Ernst were by that time taking on the bulk of the outside work at the farm. At age 64, Uncle Claus was unable to manage much of the heavy work, which continued to include grubbing the remnants of trees and brush to create more farming acreage. It might be remembered from the previous chapter that over the summer of 1904, during the last months of his life, Hinrich had worked alongside his three sons on such a task.

---

[183] The summary is taken from various sources.

Teenagers Henry (left) and Ernst took on most of the farm work after their father's death in September 1904. This photo is from around 1905, when they turned 18 and 15 respectively.

Their natural inclinations led both to pursue farming as a career. Until Henry left in 1909 for Minnesota, they ran the Oregon farm together.
Schlichting family photos

In 1904, Ernst was 14 years old and had finished eighth grade at the parochial school in Sherwood. The following year, he decided to enroll at the recently opened Concordia School in Portland. Like the proseminary in Springfield, Illinois, Concordia was an institution of the Lutheran Church-Missouri Synod. Its purpose was to provide training both for future pastors and for parochial schoolteachers. Years later, Ernst's son Erwin, and Erwin's wife Dorothy, would write, "[Ernst] went to Portland to...further his education, [but] all the while his heart was back at Sherwood."[184]

While he was at school, he wrote letters home, no doubt to his mother, but also to his brother and sisters. One letter that he wrote to his brother Henry on April 31 (sic), 1906, in English, was copied in the book *Diversity Enriches the Family*. In the letter he thanked his brother for a coat and vest Henry had sent. He asked whether Henry had gotten his stump puller, a reminder of the ongoing labor of tree removal at the farm. He passed on news of young people both he and Henry knew, then added an anecdote that revealed a humorous side for which he would become known: "...[A friend] asked me do you like college better than the farm? Then I said I like college better just for fun. And she said I think farm work is pretty dry. Then I told her sometimes it is pretty wet..."[185]

Ernst proved to be a less than enthusiastic college student. It was as his son and daughter-in-law wrote later: "his heart was back at Sherwood." Before the school year ended, Ernst was back at the farm, and there he stayed. In time, he would take on full responsibility for the farm and would continue to develop it into a successful enterprise. In the meantime, however, he worked alongside his brother Henry and, to a likely ever-decreasing extent, their Uncle Claus.

Four years later, in 1908, Henry and Ernst were managing the farm. Their mother Caroline

---

[184] *Diversity Enriches the Family History: The Schlichting Story 1914 to 1990*, p. 69.

[185] Op. cit., p. 65.

was by then 55. Sister Elizabeth was married and living in Portland. In July of that year, their sister Mary married Charles Wetzel. The young couple took up farming on property next to the Schlichting farm. This was surely a comfort to Mary's mother. Just one month later, brother John August, who had graduated that year from seminary, was married to Emma Melcher, and they moved to a remote area of eastern Washington near Odessa, where he began work in his first parish. Sister Rebecca and cousin Marie Matthiesen, then 13 and 14, had begun working in Portland, as had their older sisters, while taking turns helping at home. Theirs was a sort of job-sharing arrangement.[186]

In 1909, Caroline was the owner of the Oregon farm, while Henry (nearly 22) and Ernst (19) oversaw farm operations. However, the family still owned farm property in Minnesota. When they had moved west in 1894, they had rented it out to trusted neighbors. During the intervening years, no one from the family had been in Minnesota. In 1909 the property included:

- 168 acres, known as Parcel B, where the family had lived.
- An additional 100 acres (Parcel D) that Hinrich had purchased in 1892.

In fall 1909, Caroline purchased three smaller properties, collectively called Parcel E, directly adjacent to Parcel B and totaling 240 acres.[187]

All told, Caroline's Minnesota properties amounted to more than 500 acres.

The decision was made that Henry should return to Minnesota to tend to the property there, while Ernst would remain to care for the Oregon farm. Henry left for Minnesota in late September or early October, interrupting the journey with a visit to his brother John August and wife Emma in eastern Washington.

When Henry arrived in Jacksonville that fall, he was approaching his 22nd birthday. He settled in the house on the old home farm (Parcel B), the house where he had been born and which he had left at age six when in 1894 his parents moved to Oregon. Now returned as an adult, he wrote a letter on October 9, 1909, to his Uncle Claus in Oregon. The letter was later translated and typed in English by his brother John August, who also added a few comments—the only version of the letter that remains. At the beginning of the letter, Henry mentioned a "land deal" that was being considered. This "land deal" was the purchase of Parcel E (noted above). The purchase, made by Henry's mother Caroline, was completed on October 25.[188]

In this October 9 letter, Henry estimated that he would be back in Oregon "...after a year, after all things are in order..." But he also wrote of a growing attachment to his birthplace: "...the home and the place of my blessed father have become very dear to me. My forebears were earnest, firm and faithful people whose praise often comes to my ears. God grant that I also may become such a faithful servant of the Lord." He ended the letter with comments regarding a personal matter for Claus.

---

[186] Op. cit. p. 69.
[187] For a list of the properties the family bought and sold in Minnesota, see *Hinrich*, p. 221.
[188] Op.cit., p. 211.

When Henry returned to the Minnesota farm in 1909, he lived in the house where he had been born and raised until he was six years old. After he and Emma Reinke married in February 1911, they continued to live and farm there. Their first two children were born in the house where Henry himself had been born. In 1913 they sold this farm and purchased a farm in Mower County. They remained there and in nearby Brownsdale the rest of their lives.

This photo of the family on the Wabasha County farm was taken in the late 1880s, when Henry was a baby. Two women and three or perhaps four children, one of whom likely was Henry, are pictured in the foreground, while two men stand by horses in the background.

Photo from the Schlichting family collections

The next letter to be considered is dated March 9, 1911. It was written by Caroline Schlichting to her oldest son John August, by then a pastor and working in his first parish in a remote area near Odessa, Washington. The letter has come to us through Doris Mundhenk, one of John August and Emma's four daughters. First written in German, it had been translated by Emma's sister, Gertrude Melcher-Brandon. The original German letter is no longer present. Caroline's letter to John August and his wife Emma covered several topics:

- She voiced approval of Emma taking a teaching job, acknowledging that it would help prevent loneliness in the isolated Washington community. Likely it also was providing much-needed income.

- She wrote about Henry, who in 1909 had returned to Wabasha County, Minnesota, to see to the land the family still owned there. Although Henry's intention was to return to Oregon, his sojourn in Minnesota became permanent after he met a young woman named Emma Reinke.[189] Their wedding had taken

---
[189] Eventually each of the three brothers would marry an Emma.

The Emigrant Letters • 123

place on February 22, 1911. In this letter, written just a few weeks later, Caroline stated she was pleased that Henry was married and settled, and that he and his new wife were living on the farm near Lake City, the farm where he had been born. While Caroline likely would have preferred to have the young couple closer, she acknowledged that "It wasn't meant for him to make his home here."[190] After mentioning rising land values in Oregon, she wondered how Henry would "like it [in Minnesota]—in the long run".

- She wrote that son Ernst[191] wanted to buy a horse, seeing as the old horse, named Geisbok,[192] was no longer strong enough to pull the stump-puller cable. Ernst was building a fence which, she wrote, "will cost us a lot," and wrote that he needed to haul 140 cords of wood in summer (an immense amount). He had sowed clover along with the wheat seed as a forage crop for the following year.[193]
- She asked about little Miriam, John August and Emma's daughter, then just a toddler, and relayed word about other grandchildren and her oldest daughter Elizabeth, who had recovered from an illness.

Two letters written by Caroline in 1913 are also included in this chapter. Both regarded the marriage of her youngest daughter Rebecca to Edwin Ehlers, and both were printed in *New World Beginnings*. Only the English translations are available. Rebecca and Edwin had met when Rebecca visited her brother John August and his family in Twin Falls, Idaho, where he was serving a parish. It was at a worship service that she first met Edwin.[194] She was just 18; Edwin was 24.

Caroline wrote to Rebecca on August 17, 1913, acknowledging the plans Rebecca and Edwin had made to marry and offering careful support of them. Caroline clearly did not relish the thought of her daughter moving to far away Twin Falls, Idaho, which was Edwin's home. She ended with the request that Rebecca not set a wedding date "until we have corresponded more." The letter was placed in the *New World Beginnings* collection by Melvin Ehlers, Rebecca's son. David Schlichting noted in *Hinrich* that at the time Caroline wrote this letter, Rebecca was working in Portland as a domestic helper.[195]

On August 29, 1913, Caroline also wrote to Rebecca's fiancé Edwin: "I cannot believe that I must let Rebecca go already. It is not good that man should live alone, and if you love each other, pray that God be your constant companion through life. You have my blessing. I wish you every happiness. Remain steadfast in your faith and love..." She signed it "Mother Schlichting." Rebecca and Edwin were married on December 10, 1913, at St. Paul Church in Sherwood.

The last letter from Germany in our collection was written in 1914. While the exact date of writing is not known, the year was derived from an event noted in the letter. Special thanks to Hildegard Schmoelcke, who helped with the transcription of the German text, which is difficult to decipher. The letter was addressed to Claus and was

---

[190] Henry's return to and experiences in Minnesota, along with the fate of the family's Wabasha County properties, is discussed in *Hinrich*, Chapter 15.
[191] In March 1911 Ernst turned 21 and was running the Oregon farm on his own. Uncle Claus was still living, but at age 71 likely was no longer able to do much outside work.
[192] Geisbok had a notable place in family lore. In younger years, it seems he had been quite frisky. "Geisbok" (modern spelling *Geissbock*) is German for "billy goat," which might be a clue to the horse's nickname.
[193] Clover, a perennial crop, was sown along with wheat or oats, which are annual crops. After the grain was harvested, the clover would go dormant over winter. In the following growing season, it would grow tall enough be harvested as fodder for the animals.
[194] See *Hinrich*, pp. 202-203 for further information.
[195] op. cit., p. 203.

written by Anton Jungclaus (1858-1937). Its primary purpose was to inform Claus about his uncle, Anton Blank, who as has been noted before, was also the uncle of Hinrich, Johann II, and Rebecka Schlichting (he was their mother Elisabeth's brother).

Anton Jungclaus wrote, "Uncle[196] has not been so well this year. This past winter he could no longer walk very far, and he was so weak that he couldn't prepare his own meals. For a while a warm noon meal was brought to him. As much as possible is being done to care for him."

Beyond that news, he also described work being done in a low-lying area near Neuland called the Wild Moor. He wrote, "Sixty convicts are digging the [drainage] ditches with pickaxes. Near Vilah[197] more than 100 convicts are working on more than 40 small farmsteads. The soil is lifted by motorized machines and laid apart in rows, lengthways along the fields." What he was describing was the creation of new polders (he called them "fields") for future livestock grazing and crop growing, with drainage ditches running between them. The hard labor of digging was done by convicts, while machines provided extra power for moving the heavy soil.

At the end of the letter, Anton Jungclaus wrote, "We wish all of you the best and God's blessing. Greetings from Uncle Anton Blank."

On November 14 that year, Anton Blank would observe his 86th birthday. He lived until March 3, 1916, when he died in his 88th year, in the little house along the Oste River in Neuland that he had built more than 30 years earlier.

On May 28, 1914, John August wrote to his Uncle Claus from his new parish in Twin Falls, Idaho. The letter was typed in German, an indication that for Claus, reading German was easier than reading English.

John August thanked his uncle for a letter he and Emma had received, and he encouraged Claus, then 74, to write more: "You are now the only one of Father's family, so we should hear more from you." He wrote that he had tried to contact Claus' uncle in Germany (Anton Blank) and asked Claus for the uncle's address: "I wrote to him once before, and a younger man replied." That younger man was no doubt Anton Jungclaus, Anton Blank's nephew and writer of the 1914 letter just discussed. His reply to John August is unfortunately no longer present. It is unlikely that Anton Jungclaus' 1914 letter in our collection was a reply to John August's inquiry. It was addressed to Claus and made no mention of any letter from John August. What is notable, though, is that even as late as 1914, John August, part of the first American-born generation, was seeking contact with the last remaining family member in Germany, a man he had certainly heard about—and probably read about—but never saw.

John August was writing from Twin Falls, Idaho, where he was serving as pastor at Immanuel Lutheran Church. His primary purpose in writing was to inform Claus about the family's immediate situation. John August's sister Rebecca and her husband Edwin Ehlers—they had married the previous December—were farming near Twin Falls. Their mother Caroline was there also, visiting from Oregon. Rebecca had become very ill, and John August was unsure if she would recover. Caroline had become discouraged and was "terribly homesick," doubtless feeling torn between remaining to help care for Rebecca, while fully aware that another daughter, Elizabeth in Portland, also was seriously ill, with tuberculosis. John August knew—probably from his mother—the seriousness of that illness and commented that the doctor had prescribed fresh

---

[196] Anton Blank was uncle both to Claus Schlichting and his siblings, and to Anton Jungclaus.

[197] Whether "Vilah" is correct is uncertain; the name written in the letter is difficult to read.

air and fresh milk. His own opinion, which he wrote he had openly expressed, was that she was "too penned in and has too much work to do." (*Sie ist auch zu eingepfercht und hat zu viel Arbeit*). Elizabeth was the mother of six children, so his comment was probably correct.

At the time John August wrote his letter, Rebecca's recovery was far from certain, and he concluded by entrusting all to God's providence. Rebecca did recover. Elizabeth's condition, however, would only worsen, and she would succumb to tuberculosis on November 13, 1915, at the age of 34, leaving behind a husband and six motherless children.

This letter of John August expressed deep concern for loved ones at a crisis point in their lives. Those who experience such dark times can appreciate the anxiety and uncertainty they bring. Hopefully they also can relate to John August's expression of faith in a God who listens to prayer. A final note to any who read the letter itself: John August spelled his sisters' names in the German manner: Rebecka (for Rebecca), and Elisabeth (for Elizabeth).

The next letter in this chapter was written August 29, 1916, by Henry in Minnesota to his family in Oregon. The letter has been preserved, in English, in *Diversity Enriches the Family History*.[198] Its original is not present, but most likely it was part of the Portland collection. Whether it was first written in German or English is not known, though German is certainly possible, since Henry's mother Caroline would still have preferred receiving letters in her first language.

Henry's greeting in the letter was, "Dear ones at home." In August of 1916, those "dear ones" would have been Henry's mother Caroline and his brother Ernst. Also included would be his sister Mary Wetzel, who lived with her husband and children on a farm next to the Schlichtings. Uncle Claus had died in July of 1915 at age 75. Sister Rebecca and her husband Edwin Ehlers were farming in Idaho. Henry's cousin Marie had married Edwin's brother Emil Ehlers in June of 1915. They also were farming in Idaho.

That Henry would write "Dear ones at home" reveals the bond that held the family of Caroline and Hinrich together, one that centered on the Oregon farm. First bought as undeveloped land in 1877/1878, through years of loss and indebtedness, the land was slowly and laboriously cleared and developed into productive farmland, especially after Hinrich and Caroline and their children moved there in 1894. Their children, now adults with families of their own, continued to regard the farm as home. Throughout their lives it drew them like a magnet; indeed, *their* children, whether siblings or cousins, continued to see the Sherwood farm as a focal point and gathering destination.

---

[198] Op. cit., p. 46.

The first American-born generation gathered with their families in August 1947 for a reunion in Oregon. Pictured from left: John August, Mary Wetzel, Marie (Matthiesen) Ehlers, Henry, Rebecca Ehlers, Ernst. Their oldest sister, Elizabeth Koppelmann, had died in 1915.
Photo provided by Madeline Kingsley

Since 1913, Henry and his wife Emma had been living and farming in Mower County, Minnesota. The land the family had once owned in Wabasha County, near Lake City, had all been sold, and Henry and Emma had moved to a 160-acre farm near Waltham in that southern Minnesota county. The farm was not far from where Emma had grown up. They had married in 1911. By 1916 when Henry wrote this letter, three sons and a daughter had been born.

In December of 1913, Henry, Emma, and their first two sons travelled to Oregon by train to attend the wedding of Henry's sister Rebecca to Edwin Ehlers. On their way back to Minnesota, they stopped to visit his brother John August and his wife Emma, and their first two daughters. It was a repeat of the visit Henry had made in 1909 when he was on his trip east to tend to the Minnesota farm and property. This now was an opportunity for reunion and for Henry to bring his brother up to date on the situation in Minnesota.[199]

In this August 1916 letter, Henry sent a detailed report on the season's crops. Grain production had suffered from heat but still had fared well. Corn had grown to eight feet tall and had tassels,[200] while in the hog pasture, some stalks were as high as 16 feet. Altogether he had 27 acres of corn. He also wrote that grain threshing had taken 20 days to complete. He had hired two boys to work during that time. He also wrote that "the land boom had cooled off."

Heat had been an issue, with the hottest day reaching 101 degrees. Henry wrote, "Believe me that is hotter than 120 in Oregon. Close and sultry. Cattle also suffer from heat and do not do as well as last summer when we always had cool weather..."

Henry wrote, "Our boys (Harlan, John, and Henry) and girl (Sylvia) are in good fine health," and, "If Marie (Matthiesen) is with you give her my best regards." Whether Marie was still in Oregon is doubtful, seeing as she had married Emil Ehlers in June 1915, and the couple was living in Idaho.

---

[199] See, *Hinrich*, pp. 215-216, and *Diversity Enriches the Family*, p. 56.
[200] The tassel is the male flower at the top of the corn plant. It produces pollen to fertilize the female flowers farther down the stalk which, when fertilized, form the ears.

The Emigrant Letters • 127

Another letter, written by Henry on November 10, 1919, to his brother John August in Buhl, Idaho, has survived in its original state. Henry typed the letter, in English, on Waltham Township letterhead paper. His daughter Sylvia later wrote that he served as township clerk for some seventeen years.[201] The letter related that farm work was at its usual stage for the time of year, including threshing, silo filling, and corn shredding (for sileage).

In an effort to reduce their debt, Henry and Emma were trying to sell their 160-acre farm. Before the sale went through, they had bought an 80-acre farm and planned to move there. But the sale of the 160 acres did not go through, and they were left owning two farms. For the short term, Henry would rent out the eighty. Eventually, that 80-acre farm was sold, and Henry and Emma stayed on the 160-acre farm.

Henry related other news: Fred Schuman, a neighbor and friend from Lake City days, had been killed in an automobile crash ... His uncle, Ernst Truebenbach (a brother of Henry's mother Caroline) from Mankato, had visited. Ernst's son Herman had served in France during World War I and was back home ... Henry and his farm crew had built two silos for sileage, and that had enabled Henry to increase his cattle herd to 55 head ... He promised to send photos of the children ... He also noted that they had received John August's daughter Miriam's letter. "I shall send her $1.00 along."

In the same letter, Henry relayed, in German, a joke involving a mutual acquaintance named Knopp: "You know Knopp. He once told me, *Henrich, sag mir was der stier und das schwein ist: was das GEHLT bringt.* He was right." (Translated: Henry, tell me what a bull and a pig make: MONEY.) Judging from this and a few other letters—especially from Henry—the brothers seem to have shared a lively sense of humor.

This is the last of Henry's letters that will be mentioned. There is no doubt that many letters were exchanged among the siblings. The few listed and discussed here give us a sense of their close connection. The reader will hopefully permit me a personal remembrance. Henry, who was my grandfather, died suddenly at his home in the little town of Brownsdale, Minnesota, in September 1957. At the time I was 11 years old. My parents, my siblings and I were living on a farm just three miles east of Brownsdale, which had allowed us children frequent visits with our grandparents "in town."

In the days just before my grandfather Henry's death, three of his siblings, their spouses, and other relatives had gathered in Brownsdale for a reunion. The siblings who made the journey were Rebecca Ehlers from Idaho, John August from California, and Ernst from Oregon. It was sometime during the days of that gathering that my grandfather died unexpectedly and suddenly from a brain aneurysm. He was 69 years old. The family gathering transitioned immediately from one of sharing and reminiscing to one of shock and sorrow. His siblings remained through the day of his funeral on September 25. While much of my memory of those sad days is now lost, what I do remember is the genuine care and love they showed each other. They clearly enjoyed each other's company as they treasured those fleeting days of being together. It was obvious, also to an 11-year-old.

---

[201] *Diversity Enriches ...*, p. 55.

A rare gathering of the Schlichting siblings took place in Brownsdale, Minnesota in September 1957, where brother Henry and his wife Emma lived in retirement. The joyful occasion became a time of sorrow when Henry died suddenly at home at the age of 69. The siblings remained for his funeral service. Pictured here are Rebecca (light-colored hat), John August (bow tie), and Ernst, at right. Rebecca's husband Edwin Ehlers and John August's wife Emma are at the left. Another sister, Mary, was not at the gathering.

Source: David Schlichting photo collection

As noted above, Henry's daughter Sylvia wrote that her father served as Waltham Township clerk for 17 years. Her brother Henry—my father—wrote the following about their father for the booklet *Diversity Enriches the Family*:

"The first public work for Dad that I'm aware of was that of being a Township Clerk. I remember the large desk which was in what we called the summer kitchen. This was a good-sized room between the wood shed and the kitchen. There they would have their Town Board meetings, which no doubt would be about every month. These were to take care of business. I recall part of their job was to report all births in the township to the county recorder. Other than that, business included care and maintaining roads and bridges and weed control.

"Dad was nominated to the Mower County Farmer's Mutual Insurance Company on which he served until his death. In 1932 he was elected to be the County Commissioner for the 5th district of Mower County. He held this position until his death in 1957."[202]

Sylvia also noted that Henry was at one time asked to run for a seat in the Minnesota legislature, but that he declined.

---

[202] Op. cit., p. 45.

One Last Letter

It is fitting that the final letter considered in this work is one written by John August Schlichting. His extensive and prolific writing, commentaries, and translations have provided important information for what has been written here. On May 15, 1965, John August wrote to his sister Rebecca and his brother Ernst.[203] The date of the letter lies well outside the date range of the other letters being considered, but its retrospective view takes us 66 years back in time. A photocopy of the original was found in a box with several family documents which included the handwritten originals of Johann II's 19th century journal, and a few of John August's personal writings.

John August was 80 years old when he wrote this letter. He was living with his wife Emma in retirement in their comfortable bungalow home in Escondido, California. I was able to visit them there several times, after my family (my parents, two younger sisters, my brother and I) moved to southern California in June 1964, when I was 18. Unbeknownst to me at the time, during these last years of his life John August was engaged in a great deal of writing. This included his personal memoir, which after his death would be printed in 1991 under the title *As I Remember*, as well as a translation of Johann II Schlichting's journal. As has been noted before, John August was fluent in both German and English, and he could both read and write the old German *Kurrent* handwriting style. Early letters he wrote from school in Illinois to his parents in Oregon provide proof of that.

To his two siblings he began, "I am writing this because I feel a little homesick for your company, and, I hope, this will relieve it a little." The day he wrote, May 15, 1965, was one day after the 66th anniversary of his confirmation in 1899 at St. Paul Lutheran Church in Sherwood, Oregon. In addition to John August, the confirmands included his cousin Peter Matthiesen and a girl named Riecke Werre. He was 14 years old, and his letter transports us back to that day. He wrote with an unusual gift of clarity, sprinkled with a generous dose of humor. The day marked a solemn milestone in the lives of those teenagers, but John August also recalled the not always equally serious thinking of a 14-year-old boy. At the letter's end, he summed up elements of his growing-up years that had remained fundamental and instructive his entire life.

He recalled anxious anticipation of the confirmation rite—especially the examination preceding it—along with the many preparations made by others on his behalf. He included his sisters, brothers, and cousins as he related the celebration of the day with friends and relatives. Memories both pleasant and painful remained, all of them viewed 66 years later from the perspective of a long life well lived.

The unpleasant experiences at the parochial school at the Sherwood church could have derailed his vision to become a pastor. He had not forgotten the physical punishment meted out to the children: "A goodly number of the boys attending the German school with welts on their behind have joined the lodges. The girls took their stripes across the back without wincing. They are made a little different from the boys." This referred both to the whippings given to the children (including his own brother Henry) by the pastor, and to the church's ban on membership in any organization that involved secret rites, such as the Masons. His implication was that such harsh treatment did nothing to enhance the children's lives. They bore the physical marks of the whippings on their bodies as well as those unseen in their psyche. And in a contrary way, the whippings might even have contributed

---

[203] In 1965, Rebecca Ehlers was living near Twin Falls, Idaho. Ernst lived on the Schlichting farm in Oregon.

to the boys later joining, as men, those forbidden lodges.

Thankfully, those painful memories were overcome by the greater wisdom, devotion, and love shown him by the people most important to him. I leave it to the reader to enjoy the fullness of John August's writing skills on display in the letter. I will conclude here as he did, as he raised to the fore the people who were most important in his young life and who left a permanent imprint on him, his parents:

"My father did much to help me along spiritually. On some of the rainy days when the work was not pressing so much, he called us in and had us read from the Bible or, say, from a biography of [Martin] Luther. I recall reading along glibly one day about Luther. 'Dad, how old did Luther get to be?' 'Read that last line once more.' Here was the answer. I felt ashamed. But he did not tell me: Shame on you! Another time we were cleaning out the horse barn. I must not have been working enthusiastically. Said he, 'You have been doing quite well at school.' Of course, that was not bad to hear. But, then, came this, 'Tell me, what are traditions?' I began to deflate. 'I know what [it means], but I can't say it.' He supplied the word, 'Ueberlieferungen.' Why, of course, I knew what traditions were—things handed down.[204] And I was on top again. Dad would not belittle us but he taught us. I could go on and on. I have tried to follow that pattern. But when I asked him for permission to go to college to be a minister, he said, 'No.' His reason: 'The pastors are too quarrelsome.'[205] But we always had table prayers and we were encouraged to have our evening prayers by ourselves. Some that my mother taught me are still with me. Well, this is 66 years after confirmation and one day! I have much to be grateful for."

As has already been written, John August's father Hinrich died September 29, 1904. His mother Caroline lived more than 25 years after that until her death on March 23, 1930. She died at the family farm in Oregon and was buried beside her husband Hinrich in the cemetery of St. Paul Lutheran Church in Sherwood.

At the time of her death, Caroline's surviving children and grandchildren lived in at least four states: Oregon, Idaho, Minnesota, and California. She was the family matriarch, and while there is much less written about her than her husband, there is no question of the imprint she left on her whole family. When she and Hinrich married in July 1880, she was 27, at that time an age most would consider old for a bride. But her new husband was 43, some sixteen years older. Their maturity and considerable life experience helped shape them into a couple bonded not only by marriage vows but also by shared values, faith, and hope for the future. Their children, as they grew and matured, came to understand this and to cherish them for it. And for those of us who count ourselves their descendants today, we can hope, and strive, to live lives that reflect positively those of our emigrant forebears. For, as John August wrote in that letter, we have much to be grateful for.

---

[204] *Ueberlieferungen* literally translated means "things handed over or handed down."

[205] German: *Die Pastoren sind zu streitsuechtig.*

SOURCES

In addition to the letters themselves, the following have been used either as sources or references:

- The three-part *Johann II Schlichting Journal*. A younger brother of Hinrich, Johann wrote extensively about his childhood and young adulthood, his service in the Hanoverian army, and his harrowing voyage to America in 1866/1867. The journal then continues as a narrative of his and the family's movements and experiences after arriving in the U.S. It ends shortly before his untimely death at age 39. The journal provides a great deal of information that often helps explain matters mentioned in the letters. It also includes Johann's hand-drawn charts of family relationships, both in the U.S. and in Germany, along with charts of things like annual crop production. The journal was first translated by John August Schlichting and appeared in edited form in *New World Beginnings for the Schlichting Family* (see below). I have transcribed and translated Johann II's entire journal from his original writing. Visits to Neuland Oste Dike in 2014 and 2019 and the conversations I had with people there provided important insights for this work. For that reason, I have used my later translation throughout the book and in footnotes or references.

- *As I Remember*, by John August Schlichting (1885-1968), edited by Melvin and Hilde Ehlers, 1991. John August was Hinrich and Caroline's oldest son. Several letters are included, but equally important are the insights and memories he recorded. Only a limited number of copies was printed, but the document has been preserved and is available as a PDF.

- *Hinrich, Annals of an Immigrant Family 1866-1913*, by David Schlichting. Memoir Books, Chico, CA, 2015. This is a comprehensive study of Hinrich and his immediate family, covering the years prior to the family's emigration to America and after their arrival here. It covers roughly the same time period as our collection of letters. The book can be downloaded and read online at this web address:
https://archive.org/details/HinrichAnnalsOfAnImmigrantFamily18661913

- *New World Beginnings for the Schlichting Family*, edited by Melvin Ehlers and Charlotte Schlichting Burnett, 1989. To the best of my knowledge, this was the first attempt to collate the various writings of our 19th century forebears. It included a translation of the three-part journal of Johann II Schlichting, in edited format, as well as writings by several other family members and some early letters. It was published by the editors in limited quantity but is also available as a PDF.

- *Diversity Enriches the Family History: The Schlichting Story 1914-1990*, edited and printed by Melvin and Hilde Ehlers, with overall compilation and layout by Charlotte (Schlichting) Burnett and computer services by Melissa Holmes, 1991. A collection of writings, photos, letters, and other items, most contributors were children of the first American-born generation.

Johann II Schlichting's Journal itself, in its original form, will be donated to the Max Kade Institute for German Studies at the University of Wisconsin-Madison for permanent storage, along with a full translation. Another document containing scans of letters I have, with a typed German transcription and an English translation of each also will be donated to the Max Kade Institute.